BIBLE LESSONS

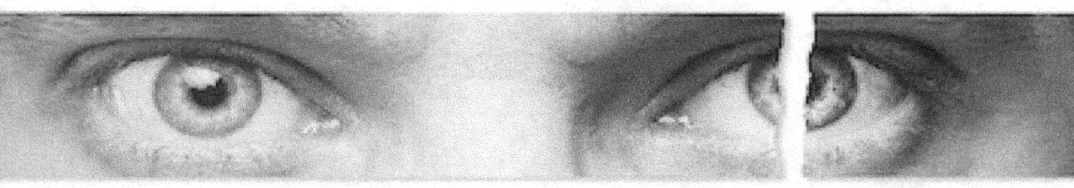

FOR BROKEN PEOPLE

BIBLE LESSONS

FOR BROKEN PEOPLE

"None were more broken than He."

William N. Bender, Ph.D.

ARPress
45 Dan Road Suite 5
Canton MA 02021
Hotline: 1(888) 821-0229
Fax: 1(508) 545-7580

Ordering Information:
Quantity sales. Special discounts are available on quantity purchases by corporations, associations, and others. For details, contact the publisher at the address above.

Printed in the United States of America.

ISBN-13:   Softcover   979-8-89330-037-6
                  eBook   979-8-89330-038-3

Library of Congress Control Number: 2024901434

TABLE OF CONTENTS

I hereby dedicate this book to a group of broken people—my Rogue Warriors—a group of men and women who have gone through hell already and survived. I can't name you here; your stories are private and shall remain so. Still, please know that I love each of you. You are the bravest folks I know, and I learned more from you than you ever did from me. May God richly bless you all and thanks!

Billy

All author proceeds from this book will go to The John Bender Foundation for further work with broken people. Please visit our website at: thejohnbenderfoundation.org

We are all broken in one way or another. Still, some are more broken than others. And if that is you, then Jesus's love and compassion speaks especially to you!

For all have sinned and fall short of the glory of God (Romans 3:23).

The Lord is close to the broken-hearted and saves those who are crushed in spirit (Psalm 34:18).

ACKNOWLEDGMENT

This series of lessons springs from my work in several areas—leading a Bible class at a halfway house for men with addictions and/or other legal problems, teaching a Sunday school class for men and women with hard, challenged childhoods, and working with teens who let weed or pills get the better of them, scaring their parents and, occasionally, their ministers nearly to death. This background provided an interesting collection of people with many challenges. And it was truly interesting for me to figure out what the Bible might say to a woman of twenty-five who was sexually molested for over a decade from the age of six or to the man who was neglected in childhood and then fought a fifteen-year meth addiction.

Folks like these are deeply broken. They have already lived in hell. However, the reality of Jesus or our personal experience of Jesus can be profoundly different for all of us. And for someone raised in a world of violence, abuse, or neglect, the first time they actually experience the love and compassion of Jesus, it is more than profound—it is life changing. I've seen it many times. It really happens.

Lives change when Jesus enters the picture, and maybe that change can happen for you. Perhaps this book can help you experience the reality of Jesus in our broken lives. We are now made whole in him. That includes you!

This book may be used as an individual study of God's Word for broken people. However, it is probably more effective when used either in one-to- one ministerial-counseling sessions or as a group study. Originally, these lessons were used in a Sunday school class as a group study, but they can be effective in any manner.

When used as a group teaching tool, I suggest spending one week on the introduction and then two weeks (two one-hour sessions on the *RogueWarrior* sections of the book by simply reading parts of that section and then asking the group "Does this sound like you?" which can encourage the openness that will foster more in-depth discussions later. While that is not a Bible lesson itself, it does set the stage for trust with Rogue Warriors. It is well worth the time.

Also, several discussion questions are presented on a work page at the end of the Rogue Warriors section. These may be used as a *homework* page for the group and then discussed in a third session if you like. You should use the level of openness among the group as the deciding factor. If they have been open with their issues in the first two sessions, then feel free to skip use of the discussion questions, and proceed to Lesson 1 during the third session.

Then beginning on week three or four, you should do one lesson each week while always asking about their relevant experiences but only if they wish to share. Encourage frank, honest discussions. Rogue Warriors will begin to trust you slowly as they realize you are genuine. God will do the rest! If you like or feel a need to do so, you should feel free to spend more than one session on a given lesson.

INTRODUCTION

A Chat with God

So there you are, sitting right there, looking at this book for one reason or another. You're probably sitting alone (given the general topic of this book; it's rather private). Maybe you are sitting at home or in a bedroom of a halfway house somewhere—maybe a local lockup. Broken folks tend to spend time in the most interesting of places, and you may even be wondering, "How in hell did I get here?"

Maybe somebody handed you this book, thinking they were offering help. Maybe they were tossing you what they consider a lifeline. You could be anywhere from fifteen to fifty, and it might be your first lifeline or merely one of many. Maybe the person that gave you this book really does give a damn about you. Of course, you can never really be sure because you, like most truly broken people, are sure of very little. We'll get into *trust issues* as the psych folks so politely put it in a while. For now just read a few more lines, and if you can, try and believe that this book might—just might—be able to help you think through a few things.

Ultimately, only you can decide if you need to change direction in life. Even teenagers sometimes need to change direction and certainly many older folks do. Lives can go wrong at any age, and many of us are broken. If things are badly broken in your life—if you're reading this at all—you might want to be open to the possibility of changing a few things. If so, then read on.

The truth is, someone is sitting there beside you. Right there on the bench or the bed or chair or wherever. God is there right now in the person of Jesus. Jesus does not abandon broken people ever—even very broken people like you. He loves us all, and once you get that, you will feel that love—yes, even you. You'll know you got that sense because you won't feel quite as lonely anymore. You might even say that broken folks are one of God's specialties!

He's sitting there with you right now. You might want to talk with him a bit or maybe not. It's really up to you, but for God's sake, don't pray! Don't toss out meaningless, grand-sounding words or memorized prayers. Nothing grandiose please. Rather, just talk with him like you would a helping friend. Just tell him what's on your mind and what's worrying you right now.

Take a few moments for that if you like. I'll wait.

Now if you actually did pray, if you did talk to Jesus, here's what Jesus might have said:

*****

Hello, my friend. Thanks for taking some time here. Now I can see you're feeling alone or maybe injured. Somehow, maybe scared. Please know that I want to care for you, and I will. But I don't want you to feel special or anything. Fact is, all of you idiots down there are broken in one way or another. Some are just more broken than others. You, in particular, have had a hard, if not impossible, life. Abused as a kid or maybe raised in a series of group homes or foster placements. Maybe you know the pain of having no family to spend a Christmas with. That's just a special kind of hell, isn't it?

Maybe you're an addict. The fun you had with weed or beer in middle school turned into a serious meth or pill addiction by the end of high school. Anyway, you're right. You're broken. It doesn't make much difference how you got broken. The only thing that matters is the depth of your brokenness, and you are already in pretty deep. But like I say, you all are broken to some extent. One of my better writers once said it best: all are sinners and fall short of the glory of God!

Still, I sure wish you would stop trying so hard to prove that damn point! Anyway, it's good to be sitting here beside you and to hear you talk to me. You haven't done nearly enough of that. In fact, I promise that if we chat a bit more, your life will change for the better. It really will. I'll make that happen. Let's just talk anytime you want.

Now don't worry, I won't hit you with all that crap about challenges in life making you stronger. You've heard all that before, and while it's true, you don't need to hear that right now. For now, just know that I'm sitting here beside you. I always do; I always will. Always. That's what I do.

Maybe we'll talk again soon, okay? I'm here when you want me. Always.

*****

Now that God has finished speaking, let me add a bit here. All of those harsh-life circumstances mentioned above lead to very bad things, resulting in very hard lives for broken people. The fun may go on for a while or at least what passed for fun when you were younger. Ultimately, though, bad decisions lead to bad outcomes. Word! You can take that to the bank!

The bad outcomes vary from one person to another but none are good. Maybe you're facing serious jail time, or maybe you are already there. You might have killed someone on the highway when you were driving drunk or tweaking, or maybe you just destroyed your family, your wife, husband, and kids. Who knows? Maybe you think you can't live without the pills or the pot. Does it really make a difference how you got this way if you're already broken?

All I know is that you're reading this for a reason. I mean, even if someone gave you this book, you still picked it up for some reason. Right?

So here's some hard truths. These, you can take this to the bank too. First of all, I'll always try to give it to you straight. I'll try and earn your respect in that way.

Next I've never been quite as broken as you probably are, and I won't pretend to be. That would be disrespectful of your struggles, and I will always respect the fight and the fighting spirit within you. I'll help you build on that.

With that said, I do understand some of what it means to be broken. Let me explain. I'm broken like everyone, but even so, I've also succeeded in many ways. I had a good family background, and as an adult, I've been successful. I've written many books over the years—

and been a respected speaker and teacher. Still, I'm broken. I failed in a couple of marriages, and I've let some people down that I love deeply. I am the typical middle kid— always in trouble and never quite satisfied, pushing boundaries particularly in my younger years. I never felt like I fit in. Does that sound like you?

More importantly, I've disappointed my family tremendously and hurt my son and my wife deeply. Perhaps, worst of all for me is knowing that both my son and my wife are much better people than I am. That really hurts. I have longed to be a better man. A better father, a better husband, brother, and son. You see, the same was true of my Dad, my Mom, and both of my brothers. They are all better people than I'll ever be. I've prayed about this for years, but I'm still the worst of the lot! Broken like I said.

Then I finally figured out that Jesus loves me anyway. Don't really know why, except that's who he is. It is what he does. Makes you wonder, doesn't it?

So that's me. Now let me tell you why you should keep reading. Several reasons, really. First you can learn something here if you want to. Just read on, and consider each lesson. If you've got a friend to do this reading with—a minister, mentor, or Christian counselor to lead you, that's great. Read and discuss this together. Still, that's not essential. You can do it alone, sitting right there where you are. It will work for you anyway if you'll let it.

Of course, I'm very confident of that because I've had the best teachers in the world when it comes to brokenness—teachers from fifteen up to forty-five or so. This includes women who were sexually molested as kids, men and women who were routinely beat up by their dad, mom, or grandparents, and men and women who know a life in and out of prison. I've come to know (and tried to help) scores of men in a halfway house and worked with many broken folks in the community over the years. I taught teenagers with severe behavioral problems—broken. These folks sometimes just seem to fall out of the woodwork with devastating needs, financial needs, chronic depression, drug dependence, a history of suicide attempts, and a complete, total feeling of aloneness. I know something about broken people, and I try to help when I can.

The next reason for you to read on: I'll break the rules. I'll tell you in these pages exactly what I think and what I know to be true about you—about broken people in general. I'll not wait until you figure it out for yourself like most psychologists have to do. I'm not a shrink, and I don't have to follow their rules. I'll give it to you straight using direct, simple terms. That's the way I think myself. I don't care if you are fifteen or eighty. Here, you will be talked to like an adult. If you are broken, you need that.

With that said, I do have a PhD in special education (the very definition of broken people) along with decades of experience with broken people. So I'll just save time and tell you what you need to know about you. No *BS!* Straight to the point. You're welcome!

Now I will need you to do one thing. I need you to test out what I say about you and discard anything that doesn't seem to fit. I know the patterns of brokenness in people and in families, and that's the basis of what I talk about here, but I don't know your particular circumstances. So it is up to you to test out what I say and know that some of this will be wrong in your case. Not all brokenness is the same, so I want you to use an idea only if it works for you. Trust your gut on what applies in your life. You'll know the truth for you when you see it.

Finally I have many years of scholarly study of the Bible. I've read it, and I know what's there. I'm not a minister, but I've discussed all the basic questions with learned men and women in college and for many decades thereafter. Further, I believe it. I know it to be true. I've experienced Jesus directly in my life. I know God, and he knows me— even old broken me. That's really something when you think about it!

Unlike most preachers, however, I'll present the Bible in its grittiest, raw form. It's a hard-hitting book really. A tough book—full of death, war, abuse, fear, betrayal, lust, destruction, and full of brokenness. It speaks very well to those raised in hell if you are willing to tackle the tough parts head-on. We'll explore what the Bible says about the hard stuff: child abuse, homosexuality, addiction, love, overwhelming guilt, forgiveness, depression, emotional pain, and all the other constellation of feelings that often seem to paralyze broken people. Just know that nothing here is sugarcoated. We'll take it on straight up; the hard facts. We'll face the tough realities. You're welcome again.

Still, please do understand that the Word of God also speaks about his profound, life-changing love, of his tenderness and compassion—things that were probably in short supply in your childhood, I'd guess. After all, that's what makes us broken. In the end, love and compassion win the day! That's what God brings to us—the very essence of Jesus is love. Don't you dare ignore that point. God's love and compassion are in your immediate future. And the blackness of emotion, the dark abiding pain you live with every day, and the ache that haunts the lives of broken people, all of that will end. Jesus, as always, said it best:

I am the light of the world; he who follows me will not walk in darkness but will have the light of life (John 8:1–3).

So that's it in a nutshell. Read this, and reflect on it, and the darkness in your life will soon be over. Just read on.

Of course, I will do my best to thoroughly introduce you to the man who is sitting right there beside you in that jail cell or the halfway house, or wherever you are. His name is Jesus, and just so you know, he once sat with the first Christians, Peter and Paul, in their jail cells too. He was right there with them every second they were in prison. He was there when they were tried and condemned for following him. He was spiritually holding their hands when they were tortured and even as they died. Jesus does not abandon broken people.

He will hold my hand too when my death comes. That is really amazing when you think about it.

If you are a believer, a Jesus follower, he will hold yours too.

So that's it. Please take this journey with me. I've been told that parts of this book have changed lives, and I believe it can change yours. As one example, let me tell you about sitting on my back deck one afternoon with a recovering meth addict who flat out told me she could trust no one. That she'd never had a healthy sexual relationship in her life. That she was always angry. And that her whole life was *shit*! (her words). The fact is, at that moment, she was right.

This woman was in deep clinical depression and was sure she would fail in her attempt to complete many requirements of Accountability Court (a non-incarceration sentence for drug involvement that includes police monitoring of her behavior rather than lockup). She also wanted to get her kids back from foster care and put together her family once again. But she feared failure and trusted no one to help including me.

I didn't respond directly. I just handed her the Rogue Warriors section of this book and asked her to read two paragraphs—only two—the part about pride preventing folks from seeking and receiving help. I wanted her to accept my help and to be open to it. I wanted her to know, really know, Jesus, and I also wanted her to know I'd dealt with folks in her situation before. So she read those two paragraphs, but then when she finished them she didn't stop—she just kept on reading. I just sat there, silently watching.

Then I saw a single tear roll down her cheek. She read on as she cried. She read the document all the way to the end, then she looked at me and simply said, "That's me. That's exactly me."

That day at that moment, Jesus changed her life. She opened up to accept the help she needed. This book—that one section of this book—helped her in that regard to be open to the possibility of help. Over the next six months, she did rebuild her life. Finishing Accountability Court requirements, she got her kids back. They are now together as a family. They all go to church with my wife and I most Sundays when she is not working. She now knows God.

There are many other examples like this. Jesus can rebuild lives that are broken, no matter how broken, including yours. Still, rather than present other stories here (and knowing all about your trust issues), I'll let you—in fact, I'll encourage you—to decide for yourself what Jesus can do with your life. Just read on!

Anyway, from one broken person to another, Godspeed to you, and I do hope this helps you a bit.

Billy

Rogue Warriors

William N. Bender

In late January of 2017, I went rogue. I created a Sunday school class in the balcony of our church. It was the only empty space I knew of on Sunday morning. I did that with no permission whatsoever because I felt I had to. The plain fact is our church was filled with a bunch of Christians who had been seeped in Christianity all their lives. Most came from good families— these were and are some of the best people I know. However, our church had nothing to offer folks whose lives were truly broken. We had no specific Sunday school class for folks like some of you—folks who have already lived in hell. Of course, Jesus was there in that church, and Almighty God was worshiped there, but we still didn't have the class that these broken folks needed.

Several of these broken folks were raised in hell, and I had five deeply broken people ranging in age from eighteen up to thirty-six coming the very next Sunday! I'd invited them to come, so I had some serious responsibility there, and the possibility of officially creating a new Sunday school class (I feared) had to go through time-consuming committees, etc. I needed an appropriate class in four days!

So I went rogue. I needed a quick Bible-based lesson on feeling harshly judged when one was going to church. This was one of their biggest concerns. They'd all told me they would probably feel *judged* if they even went to church! I needed a lesson on that topic (Feeling Judged: A Reality Check). I needed one on why church attendance was worth it (God's Promises to Us) and another class on dealing with overwhelming, paralyzing guilt (How Guilty Am I?). What's worst, I needed those lessons right then! So I talked with my wife, and we prayed. God seemed to be saying, "Just do it!" So I created those lessons, and I taught them to my five guests (these broken people) over the next three weeks.

After that, I went to my pastor, a man I deeply respect and confessed to going rogue. I apologized and explained why I'd done it. I promised to never do it again. He then smiled and said, "I saw you guys up in that sanctuary balcony during Sunday school time. I started to go up, but I figured something important might have been going on. I guess it was. Okay, so now I think we've got a new Sunday school Class."

May God be praised for that man, for his decision, and for all that has come out of that! Men of God often show great wisdom, and in that case, he did!

During that rogue period, I wrote down a few thoughts presented below about and for those broken people. This section below on Rogue Warriors was never intended to be a Sunday school lesson, and I was not sure I would even show it to anyone when I wrote it. Still, I did, and I've found that this is the best place to begin with broken people.

Now if you are sitting alone in a jail cell or in a halfway house somewhere, or merely in your own bedroom at home, just read this Rogue Warrior section and reflect on it a bit. See if this description fits you, and if so, what fits and what doesn't. If you're doing this as a group study, and I hope you are, then discuss those points together over the next few days.

I don't mean to waste your time here, but other broken people have said this is important stuff, so take as long as you like with this. Maybe it can open your thoughts a bit.

Night Thoughts on Broken People from a Long Sleepless Night

So this zat 4:34 a.m. on February 2, 2017. We'd begun to meet in the church balcony on Sunday morning—three women and two men—broken people from the school of hard knocks! They each knew hell intimately. They were broken just like me. Reflecting on what we might call ourselves (having rejected "The Balcony Bunch)," I began to think of who they are or who we are. As you can see, that led to an absolute seizure of writing. These are my notes to them, to you, and to myself. I hope some of this helps, but why in all that is holy did this have to happen at 4:34 in the morning?

I began to think of common traits, if any, that victims of abuse and/or of addiction might share, but there's the first problem. I hate the terms *victims of abuse* and *victims of addiction*. The folks I have come to know are anything but *victims*. They may have made a few bad choices or maybe even many bad choices, but they are not victims. I don't like *survivors* either. They are living and moving on with life—doing much more than just surviving. While many of their attitudes and self-perceptions are predicated on having suffered abuse or gone through years of addiction, their past history of abuse does not define them. These folks are much more than victims or survivors. They have seen the enemy, they looked into the pit, and they lived there. Some were born there. They know the depths of hell and of total despair. They've seen into the eyes of evil incarnate. And the truth is, they've survived. At the very least, they were not destroyed! Most are struggling with their personal demons still.

They have many scars, but they came through alive. They remind me of the Knights Templar of old—warrior brothers (and sisters) who fought, bled, fell, and got up again and again. They survived with their many battle scars. The scars are different for each one but all have them. I have a few myself but nothing like these guys. They are braver than I'll ever be. These guys are pure warriors—the best term I can come up with. This is going to be fun. May God help us in this! I hope I don't screw this up!

Despite having gone through the worst abuse imaginable (at least some of them), there is a spark of hope here—a fierce pride, some type of light deep in their soul, and even the darkest depths of despair. If they have seen evil up close, they have also seen something else.

Be still and know that I am God!

The last thing these guys want is pity. Clearly, there is something to build on here, and that is why most of these guys are succeeding; most are moving forward in life. Those that aren't were not invited to come with us up here to the balcony. My thoughts and prayers for those several that I didn't invite up here to join us. Some folks just didn't seem to be ready, and I made the call on who to invite. It was mine alone. May a merciful, loving, benevolent God forgive me if I was wrong in even one instance there!

So what does define them? Who are they as a group? While all their situations are different, and each individual is different, are there common issues here and common traits? I'm usually pretty good at seeing who people really are, and I've studied psychology, personality, character traits, temperament, and an array of mental health problems for decades. Still with these guys, I didn't feel that I'd gotten a full and complete handle on it. That's probably why I'm writing this—to clarify some thoughts.

These guys often surprised me, and for a simple mind like mine, they fit into no clear category. Still, I thought I saw some things that most of them, certainly not all, have in common. So here are the thoughts for whatever they may be worth.

First these guys in general begin to believe their abusers in a deep sense. They begin early on to think that the verbal abuse or physical abuse they went through tells them who they really are—that's Stockholm Syndrome at its finest. The physical and emotional abuse they endured is deeply internalized, and they somehow think they might have deserved it. This is the darkness inside them: a blackness that covers their joy. They feel unworthy. They even identify with their abusers and often want to *forgive* them. They believe that if anybody really knew them deep down, they couldn't possibly love them. They believe on some levels that they are unworthy of love and of happiness. This has led to suicide attempts for most of them, though not all.

This interior darkness leads to horrid life decisions. For example, in most future relationships, broken people will never give of themselves fully. They never open up. Further, they will almost always choose other abusers in future relationships, and thus, continue the pattern to affirm who they believe they are—an unlikable, unlovable, unworthy person. That only stops when they intentionally, through strength, integrity, spiritual development, maturity, and self-knowledge (as well as great effort) break that pattern. Some make that journey successfully while others do not.

Because they do internalize their past history of abuse and tend to believe deeply in their own worthlessness, many of them get really, really pissed off. They are angry. They are viciously angry at the world in general, and that transfers to almost anyone they come into contact with. When they point that harsh light of anger at you, you should run! Run far and fast, and stay gone for a while. If you are wise, you will come back. And when you come back, you will be quite humbled. That's the only way back in with these guys—being humble—and even then, you won't get very far in.

I have come to see that the anger comes from some spark, some faded light of hope within them, and some sense that they are not who their abusers have told them they are. That spark is their pride—the good side of pride. The pride that helps one survive the harshest circumstances. Pride can help one survive hell. Maybe that kind of pride is God's small voice on the inside; Jesus speaking if you will.

It is their pride reaching out and trying to survive. There seems to be this ongoing constant battle inside them. They believe they deserved the abuse, yet on another level, they know they didn't, that they are much more than that. That internal battle keeps these guys emotionally exhausted.

They see others as clueless to their internal struggles. In general, they are right. Thus, beyond general, meaningless, shallow conversation, most others are unworthy of their time. That is why most *Bible Bangers* fail to reach these broken people. Energetic religious folks, seeped in Christian teachings for their entire lives, may very well be *on fire for God*, but in general, most simply don't understand this total brokenness very well. You can't just *save* someone existing in a parallel universe. A hearty handshake and a Biblically based smile—what I call the Great Christian Grin—leaves these folks cold. A Baptist with a five-minute testimony or a couple of Jehovah's Witnesses with a smile and a Bible at the door can't touch these guys.

I'm not saying here that these things don't change lives—they often do. I'm just saying that for this batch of very broken people, much more will be needed. You have to get real with these guys. Talk to them, listen to them, tell them your failures, and even get dirty with them. Drive them to court dates. Learn of their felonies and misdemeanors. Learn the lingo. Most of all, use their language including all the words not usually heard in church. Make just a bit of an opening there, and God will step in! Jesus will use the smallest open door to touch their soul, and he'll worry about their language (and yours) later.

Some of these broken folks had *partners* in and during their abuse—siblings who suffered with them with the same abuse. I've seen that once or twice before. Those partners become soulmates, bonded together through unimaginable horrors, like men in battle, and like men at war, those partners provide strength to each other. They are deeply bonded for life. No one else will ever touch—no one else will ever come close—to the depth of that relationship, and no one should try. Those partners provide a strength to and for each other more profound than death itself—brighter than the sun. There is great strength there, but you, as an outsider, will never control that strength. They won't share control of that bond nor should they. It is theirs alone. Do watch that bond carefully, and when private communion begins between the partners, know enough to shut up and get the hell out of the way. Important stuff, good stuff, and even great stuff can and does happen at that point even with no guidance from you.

Broken people will not trust you, unless you earn their trust through unimaginable time and effort. Few make that effort; fewer still have the time.

You will never earn their trust. They really don't trust. Suck it up, and live with it. Not everything has to make sense. It's really not about you.

You will never earn their trust, so don't try. Of course, you should always, always, always try. What are you here for—what am I here for if not to try, right?

They will relate together quite normally. They can and do relate to others quite normally. For them, it is a *show* or pretense, but let's get real for a minute. Maybe a certain pretense is the basis of most social interaction for all of us. When we casually say to someone, "How are you today?" Do we ever really care?

Broken people quickly ascertain whether you are *of* them or not. When they run you away, you should come back. You should always come back. Generally, they are okay with it, and if not, trust me, they will let you know. Go away at that point, but come back. Always, always, always come back.

They judge often harshly and, sometimes, cruelly but usually quite accurately. They have a great built-in *BS* detector and zero tolerance for phony relationships.

They can smell a phony person from across the room. If that harsh, cruel judgment falls on you, run for your life.

They do not, not ever, respect a phony. We (those of us whom they perceive as nonbroken people) are all phony. We are presumed to be phony, unless we are one of them.

We will never, ever, be one of them.

They lie. They tend to lie somewhat less than the average Joe Blow, but they do lie.

Broken people never ask for help. Even when they know they should and truly believe they will get it, they don't ask. When they need it, they never ask for help. When they want it, they never ask for help. When they know help is available that someone really wants to help, they never ask for help. So here's some big damn news: they never ask for help!

Asking for help actually hurts these guys. When fierce pride is all you have, then that fierce pride is what you cling too. That is the dark side of pride—it holds help far away. So they never ask for help! Now I realize how stupid I've been on that score in hoping that they would begin to ask for help. Then again, I've been stupid before. This batch ain't my first rodeo, and these guys won't be my last. I'll find another batch of misfit warriors, and I'll be stupid again. I'll make many of the same mistakes again, trust me!

Some of them, on the rarest of occasions, ask for help. Didn't I mention surprises before? Sometimes I think these guys are the walking dead—emotional eunuchs that can't possibly survive. They show no emotion. They share nothing. They celebrate no achievements at all! Pride—the dark pride can mean indifference even to positive things in life. How in hell are these guys succeeding at all?

Sometimes they look like they can't love. That they can't feel. Those emotional walls helped to protect them. They still protect them, protected their core: their deeper self during their sojourn in hell. The fact is, they feel love deeply. They are overly sensitive to any criticism because they feel everything deeply. That is why they withdraw from the world. Some of them actually hibernate (I had one of those up in the balcony)! Of course, they desire most of all—acceptance and even respect, but certainly not pity.

They know they have worth, and they know they have more wisdom in their little toe than most of us acquire in a lifetime. They have lived in hell, and most of us haven't. That's why the rest of us seem clueless. We aren't dumb—they don't see us as dumb—just clueless.

They don't communicate with those of us deemed unworthy of their time. In fact, none of us are deemed worthy of their time.

They never apologize, not ever—even when they should. It is a sign of weakness. Their dark pride means they can show no weakness!

They really are seeking growth, seeking God, or seeking something meaningful in life. They want something greater than the pain or greater than what they have felt before. They want things to make sense. They want a good life, a reason to exist. That is why some of them—the female warriors have babies—they create someone to love. That is why others tend to seek relationships, most of which, will fail because of their emotional self-protective walls. If you won't or can't give yourself completely to someone else, should you pretend to give yourself at all? These guys try and try again in relationships that are doomed based on their inability to open up.

That desire to be open to others is the key if there is a key. There is room here for emotional growth and even spiritual growth, perhaps for the Spirit of God. Some broken folks know God while some don't but all are seeking.

I really hope I don't screw this up. Much can be accomplished here if I don't screw this up.

They are all stronger than me.

They are stronger than most folks I know. They are warriors. I seem to keep coming back to that. I don't know if that's the name we need or not, maybe a bit too militaristic for some. Ultimately, they will decide on their name. The world, the universe owes them that, at least that.

What I do know is they have a story to tell, probably more than one. They have much to teach us—we who are clueless to what adversity really is.

So now it's 6:52 a.m., and Wify sets her alarm for 7. My day begins. Our pawed friends go out, I turn the coffee on. Time for me to get my sorry self up and take the lady her coffee while she's still in bed. She deserves it.

Not sure if writing this was worth it, but maybe it was. Who knows? Maybe I'll share this with you guys up in the balcony. If I do, then I hope it makes sense or maybe made you think a bit. Please don't take anything to heart here, unless you think it fits. I can be wrong and, many times, I am, at least as often as I'm right. If you like, mark this up and give it back to me. Tell me if a paragraph really spoke to you, if it is on the money. Then put a big *BS* beside the sections that are just plain wrong, but do tell me why. Please explain if you can. I do want to understand. Maybe some of this even made you smile.

I should have phoned every one of you, Jokers, at 4:34 a.m. just to make your phone ring that early! Do you see the crap you guys put me through?

Anyway, I love you guys—every one of you, sorry broken guys. I'll see you next Sunday up in the balcony. I'm looking forward to it.

Note: The final name of our group, *Rogue Warriors,* was selected by the group in late February of 2017 after I shared this document with them. Some were already Christians. One or two were not, but they were all rogues, and they were certainly all warriors. They've made it through hells that few of us will ever know. They've earned the honor of that title. This world owes them at least that much!

These guys really are the bravest folks I know! They are my superheroes! With Jesus right there beside them, they will surely succeed. May God smile on our upcoming discussions and our joint battles.

Discussion Points on Rogue Warriors

- Did this document describe you in any way? How? Do you trust? Are you paralyzed by pride? How does this fit who you are? Look over the points again if you'd like.

- It might help you to identify three sections or paragraphs in that document that most touched you? Reflect on why?

- Do you need to seek more religion in your life? Have you ever been religious before? Would you be better off with more spiritual depth in life?

- Could more involvement in church—if you can find a good one where folks are right up front and honest about things help you? How?

- Have you ever studied the Bible, specifically looking for lessons on being broken before? What does the Bible say about abuse or addiction or guilt?

- Some emotional states do paralyze us. Things such as anger, guilt, negative judgements, hatred, or fear. Given the range of negative emotional states, which of these comes closest to what you feel? What describes you?

- Have you ever prayed before? Does Jesus just seem like a fairytale for idiots or weak-minded people? Do you know Jesus personally?

Lesson 1

Feeling Judged! A Reality Check!

"**I** walk into a church, and these Bible Bangers immediately judge me. Pisses me off! They have no clue!"

Do you feel like that? Do you feel harshly judged just because you walk into God's house? Maybe your tattoos or piercings *give you away* as being different. Do you feel as if everybody is looking at you when you go into a church?

Here's a question. How did your addiction or maybe a nontraditional upbringing prepare you for looking different? Did your background leave you feeling judged wherever you go? Is being judged only something you feel at church?

Such feelings of being judged are often experienced by addicts in recovery or victims of abuse. One reason that NA and AA classes work for so many is that in that context, there is usually no judgment—all are welcome. It should certainly be that way in God's house too!

Jesus Standing Between Us and Judgment

So we'll start with that. Let's begin with Jesus. Let's consider how Jesus responded to harsh judgment of the religious leaders of the day. The best example is found in John 8:1–11.

This is the familiar story in which Jesus saved a condemned woman's life with one wise statement: "Let he who is without sin throw the first stone." Now today we know that Jesus and God are one, but it helps to also remember that in his time, he was viewed merely as a traveling Rabbi. He would have known Jewish law intimately, but the crowd and religious leaders were correct—the woman should have been stoned to death, according to Jewish law. Yet here, Jesus did not blindly follow the law. He found a way to show love, compassion, and mercy while still emphasizing the point of the law. He then told her to, "Go and sin no more."

In fact, in this example, it is not an overstatement to say that Jesus stood between that woman and the harsh judgment of those religious leaders. Of course, he does the same today. If you feel judged when you go to church, imagine Jesus standing right beside you (he is, you know) and shielding you from harsh judgments of foolish, sin-filled Christians. Remember, they are broken too!

Is My Background a Blessing?

Harsh judgments often result from harsh backgrounds, and while no one wishes a horrid background on anyone, there are other ways to view your own past. Here are a few questions for those with nontraditional and nonChristian backgrounds.

First what is the single biggest blessing God has given you? While we can certainly list the negatives resulting from addiction, abuse, neglect, or family hardship, are there positive results that we can list? Here are some possible ideas.

Do we, who are in recovery, know things others don't? Have we experienced things that others haven't, and what did those experiences teach us? Have we something, perhaps some wisdom or insight, to share in the broader Christian community? What would we say to a struggling single mom who wandered into church? To a recovering drug addict? To a pregnant fourteen-year-old girl? Would our input be different from what some other Christians might say? Do we have any strengths arising from our harsh background that we can bring to others?

Given a nontraditional family background or a history of abuse or addiction, what do we experience when we come to church? Do we experience something different from those who were raised in church? Do we experience Jesus's love as we would if we'd been in church all our lives? Do we see/experience harsh judgment because of who we are?

Do we experience joyful acceptance from others? Do we feel we have to hide who we are?

Did We Judge Others First?

What did you expect when you came to church? Did you expect to be judged? Was that fair to those already coming to church? In fact, did we judge Christians before Christians judged us? How are we judging the Christians in this church right now? Is that a harsh judgment? Is that fair? Please know that there will always be a biblical challenge in these lessons. I promised you the hard truths, and that is one. The challenge will usually cause us all to look at ourselves; that is the richness of the Jesus's teachings throughout the Bible.

Of course, it is a fact that most study guides used in churches are written by lifelong Christians, and for lifelong Christians. So we might ask, what can those lessons teach broken people? Are those lessons even relevant? While these tools are wonderful for those seeped in Christian love and the doctrines of the church, these lessons are probably not the best way to introduce Jesus to us broken people from a nontraditional background. How, then, do we begin to experience the love of God as manifested in Jesus's compassion? What does that mean for us?

Judgement and Responsibility to Judge

Here are several other Bible lessons on harsh judgements. First Romans 2:1 says, "Judge not, least ye too be judged." Also read Mathew 7:1–5. Based on these passages, who is allowed to judge others? Who is allowed to judge you? Do we judge others sometimes? Are we allowed to?

How about me judging myself? How about that paralyzing guilt that self-judgment sometimes brings? Is that experience the will of God? Don't I have to judge me to be honest with myself? Am I harder on myself that I am on others? Many broken people are.

Most folks miss the idea that according to the Bible, we are not supposed to even judge ourselves. With the common element of being abused in some fashion, how likely are we to judge ourselves harshly? Is God's instruction wise for broken people?

Of course, we must realize that judging ourselves is different from carefully considering our actions in light of God's Word. We are instructed to evaluate our actions and make decisions about how to move toward God's will in our lives. Still, these are Christian decisions made in love for our growth in God's will, not harsh judgments of others. Big difference!

Why Make the Effort?

So if I get judged by others, why do it? Why go to church at all? Why show up? This is a question every Christian asks himself in one form or another. "Why get up this morning for church when I'm so tired?"

"Can't I just go fishing today or do something I enjoy?"

While there are many reasons to go to church, worship is the primary reason. Our purpose in life is to worship God, and thereby, live within his will. We strive in worship to get closer to God. That is our purpose and reason for existence. Still there are other reasons, and some of these may also be very important for us Rogue Warriors. Here are a few.

I need the peace of mind promised by God to me.

I want my kids to grow up in a safe, middle class, loving home even though I didn't. My kids need to be in church and to see me in church.

My husband/wife can maintain sobriety better with God in his/her life.

I'll support that.

I want to rejoin our common community and not feel so alone all the time. I deserve to be a member of God's family.

In deciding to come to church and in dealing with the feeling that others may judge you, even though they shouldn't, we should prayerfully consider each of the reasons above, and that should help us make the effort to be in God's house.

So How Do I Respond When Feeling Judged?

So how should we respond when others who are failing to follow God's mandate to "judge not" do, in fact, judge us? What do you think would be Jesus's response to that? Of course, they shouldn't judge us, but other Christians are still human, and therefore, they are sinners. Some will judge you. That's a fact. So here are some strategies that can help.

Use our thoughts. Talk ourselves through it! Talking to ourselves when we confront any negative emotion (like our unease when we feel judged) is a powerful tool. One former addict shared this trick with me at a halfway house one evening. When feeling judged, merely say to yourself, "I'm sure glad that you are not my savior!"

Pray! Prayer can help, and even quick silent prayers reach Almighty God.

"God, thank you for loving me even with my past. Thank you for being more loving than some of your followers, and thank you for forgiving me! Now please help me to forgive them."

Read! The Bible helps in many instances. Use these passages along with the ones previously mentioned. Seek the assurance in Romans 8:31; Romans 8: 37–39; and John 3:16 (and in that last single verse substitute the word *me* for *the world*. Then read it again.).

Be Faithful to God and Always Present in His House! The more folks see you in church, the less judged you will feel! Even those that did judge you initially will do so less and less as they see your commitment to God in your continuing presence. Thus, be faithful and ever present in God's house! You will then be rewarded beyond measure!

LESSON 2

God's Promises to Me!

Okay, so maybe we can get over the being judged part. At least over time maybe we can. Still, here's a question, why should we? Why should I be a follower of Jesus? Why get up early and go to church on Sunday? Why bother at all? Can't I just try to be a nice person and care for my family and others without worrying about Jesus? Isn't being a nice person the only real moral code for life?

Is it possible that a belief in Jesus does more than make me a good ethical person? What, in hard terms, does God do for me? What exactly are God's promises to me?

One quick answer. Many addicts swear that Jesus helped them get sober and stay that way! Now we can assume they are all weak-willed idiots, or we can consider the possibility that they are on to something here. We know that getting clean and staying that way are not simple things, so maybe we should be open to that possibility of God's help. That's one reason to get to God's house every Sunday. At least for a few Sundays. Maybe we experience something like this.

Still, there are other reasons to get closer to Jesus. For example, while God makes many promises to Christians, two are critical. God promises:

A life everlasting in the presence of God and a mental peace that passes understanding.

On Life Everlasting

Romans 6:23 teaches us about the consequences of sin and shows us one of God's promises to us. "For the wages of sin is death; but the gift of God is eternal life through Jesus Christ our Lord."

Clearly, Paul, the writer of Romans, speaks of God granting Christians an eternal life through Jesus, and that is comforting. Personally, when my dad was dying in 2017, his faith helped him immeasurably. He knew he was going to see Jesus! Further, when he passed away, it helped me and my brothers, knowing that he was with God.

Still a higher authority than Paul was Jesus himself. One of Jesus's final statements on the cross was a statement on everlasting life. His words to the criminal who was tortured and killed beside him clearly show the promise of eternal life with God. "Today you will be with me in Paradise" (Luke 23:39–43).

On Inner Peace

Christians talk of heaven all the time. In fact, of these two promises, the life everlasting promise is the promise most frequently emphasized. However, sometimes we overlook the fact that Christians find that the peace in this life right now is peace of mind. For we broken people, isn't that a more critical promise?

Let's reflect a bit. Doesn't life defeat us all at times? Doesn't life crush us all? Have you ever had something so negative happen that you felt at the end of your rope? Does this seem to happen daily? Was there a horrible decision in court against you? How about a horrible embarrassment resulting from yours or a family members' bad decisions? Have you ever known the death of a child, the death of a parent, or sibling? A divorce? Have you ever been so angry you cursed at God?

Life Happens!

Psychologists call these major changes in life *stressors*, and they can be positive, life-changing events (marriage, birth of a child, or last child leaving the home) or negative stressors (divorce, death of a child or family member, life-threatening disease, or getting fired from the job). These are all major stressors in life and seem to happen every two to five years for folks between eighteen and twenty-five or so. There are just more major changes in life during the early years. After that, according to psychologists, adults have one of these major stressors every decade or so. Personally, I've had a higher frequency than that.

In that sense, everyone needs the peace of God, particularly in difficult times of life. Can you use that peace in your life right now?

So here's the big question: given that all lives have stressors and yours may have more than the usual number, is it still possible to find the peace God promises? When we crash or freeze up in life, will a solid belief in God's promise of peace help?

Simple answer: yes!!! In fact, God's Word will help. Here's a quick example. In your Bible, read Psalms 23. That's a very familiar Psalm, and if you read it out loud, slowly, you will actually feel stress leaving you. This is more than the meaning of the words. It is the fact that *that* passage is so specific it will relax you a bit even when you are stressed to the max!

Read it again (the whole Psalm). Read it slowly, and see if you feel that. Now consider the works of the Psalm. Can those assurances help when you face an impossible situation?

My Family Passage

Here's a personal example. Psalm 121 is and has been a favorite of my family for the last several generations. My great-grandmother died well before I was born, but family tradition holds that she read this regularly when she lost a child and when she gave birth to one (she had thirteen kids—she was doing something right and apparently very frequently!) It should come as no surprise that when my wife and I lost our twins in the womb, we turned to this passage and found comfort. When my mom died, I also used our traditional family chapter.

Read Psalm 121 slowly and reverently. It will bring God's peace to your soul. There are many other statements of God's peace in the Bible. Christians read any or all of these in difficult times. This is inner peace—a peace that is not changed even when harsh life situations come into our life. As another example, read Romans 8:11 or Romans 8:37–39. Also, 1 Corinthians 13 is a favorite. Spend some time. Read these, and see if you feel your stress go down!

Where Do I See the Peace of God?

Here is solid evidence of a man experiencing God's peace in an impossible life situation. Paul was in prison (and Roman prisons were not *country club* jails—they were the hardest of hard times). Still, his sense of the closeness of Jesus was so profound that while in prison, he wrote several letters of encouragement to other Christians (see Philippians). In that book, he sang the praises of Jesus and his church and talked of "Peace that passes understanding..." (Philippians 4: 4–7).

Some Bibles have a scholarly introduction about the books in the Bible. If yours does, you might read the intro to Philippians about his prison letters.

What kind of courage is this? What kind of peace of mind is this that when Paul is in prison, he writes of deep, inner peace and love of Jesus? How does someone in that situation write encouragement to others? Clearly Paul had deep inner peace.

Summary

So the question is: do you have that kind of inner peace? Do you want that? This is a deep foundation of peace that can be the foundation for change in your life. It is truly a peace that passes understanding.

Now you tell me. Which of these promises is immediate? Life everlasting or inner peace right now? Which is most important to you right now?

I'll bet I know the answer. When you chat with God again, feel free to ask him to bring you that inner peace, then read Psalms 23 again slowly. You'll feel it. Word!

LESSON 3

My Higher Power Is Jesus

Okay. Now we'll talk basics. I have had a few Rogue Warriors that were not Christians, so let's deal with the basics of Christian beliefs.

Who is Jesus, and what does he mean to me? Is there anything of substance here other than some fairytale or some imagined God? Is this stuff just wishful thinking? Is God real?

Can Jesus be my higher power? Will a practice of faith in Jesus really change my life? Has it changed others or are all those folks just delusional? Is that what higher power means? Is this stuff even real? Did God really enter history in the person of Jesus? If so, why was he tortured to death? What was that torture like? Why did he die? How did he die for us? How did that help me?

What did Jesus say about who he was? "I am the light of the world" (John 8:12)…and what exactly does that mean? How did Jesus intervene with God for us? What exactly do Christians' believe about Jesus?

Here's a simple answer: Jesus is a manifestation of God through which God intervenes directly into history. Jesus was both man and God, and he shows us how to live a life of love, compassion, and inner peace if we can learn to live as he did. By his death, Jesus paid a price for our sins, for each one of us, and thus, he recreated our perfect relationship with Almighty God.

The Roman Road

The Roman Empire ruled the world for nearly five hundred years, and they tied their empire together with a road system leading everywhere! They built the best roads in ancient history with many layers of rock, sand, and cover stones. Many of those roads and some of their bridges are still in use today thousands of years later. Roman roads were perfect roads, deeply lined with rock that lasts forever. They were in that sense everlasting. That's why the concept of the Roman Road is used by many Christians to explain the context of fundamental Christian beliefs.

In this context, the Roman Road refers to an ordered set of Bible verses from the book of Romans that states Christian belief in a nutshell. While different folks site different specific verses, almost all follow this general set of verses to explain Christian beliefs. Here they are.

Romans 3:23 "For all have sinned, and fall short of the glory of God" In this world, there is no one who is innocent. "All fall short..."

Now here are a few reflection questions for you to challenge yourself with. Do you think you are innocent? Do you think you are a good person in general? Do you believe what others believe about you? How much do your early-life experiences influence what you believe about who you are?

Paul then talks of what we all deserve.

Romans 6:23 "For the wages of sin is death; but the gift of God is eternal life through Jesus Christ our Lord." The punishment that we have earned for our sins is death. But Paul doesn't mean just a physical death but an eternal death! This is a total absence of God in our lives! Still, note the last half of that verse above. "But the gift of God is eternal life through Jesus Christ our Lord."

God has forgiven us as a gift paid for by Jesus himself. This forces the question, have you been honest with yourself about your sins? About how good a person you really are?

Romans 5:8 "But God demonstrates His own love toward us, in that while we were still sinners, Christ died for us." Jesus's death paid for the price of our sins. Jesus's horrible death and his resurrection proves that God accepted Jesus's death as the payment for our sins. What type of love is this?

Romans 10:9 "If you confess with your mouth Jesus as Lord, and believe in your heart that God raised Him from the dead, you will be saved." Because of Jesus's death on our behalf, all we have to do is believe in him, trusting his death as the payment for our sins—and we will be saved! What does being saved mean? How does this confession of Jesus as Lord of my life bring me peace? Can it? Has it worked for other broken people?

Romans 5:1 has this wonderful message, "Therefore, since we have been justified through faith, we have peace with God through our Lord Jesus Christ." Through Jesus Christ, we can have a relationship of peace with God. This is the peace that passes understanding.

Finding God's Peace

So ask yourself. Are you willing to believe in a risen Jesus? Is he your higher power? I'd suggest that he is regardless of whether you acknowledge him or not. In fact, you can prove that to yourself. If you do begin to talk to him a bit through prayer, you will begin to find his peace in your soul, and your mind will begin to be more at rest. Try it. After all, you are already pretty broken and really have nothing else to lose.

Still, I can hear you asking where is this peace of God for me? We asked the same question in the last lesson too because it is an important question. It is a critical one, and I wanted to talk about it again because the Roman Road is a slightly different approach to the question of inner peace.

First are you honest enough to admit that you don't really feel that inner peace right now? If so, then ask yourself these questions. Where do I get that peace? Where do I see this peace of God? Where do I see God's love? What's the evidence? Where have I felt God's love? Where do I see in others God's love?

Acting Like Jesus

In short, this peace comes because of God's grace. It was a gift for us all shown in Jesus's death and resurrection. Still, you'll experience it more directly when you begin to act like Jesus acted—loving, forgiving, open to life, and caring for others. Here's a few questions to think on.

Do I act like Jesus? Have I ever? Can I?

Where have I shown God's love to someone today? Have I done something nice for anyone else today?

Where do I show his compassion? What caring do I show others on a regular basis?

Do I invest time and money making lives of others better? Do I give of myself?

Is Jesus a real entity in my life? Is he there in my mind right now? Is his compassion profound enough to change who I am? To combat my addiction or the pain of my troubled upbringing?

Finally, do I show God's love? When I do, is that God in me? Is that Jesus in me?

Meditate on these questions quietly. In fact, I'd suggest you ask yourself these questions daily for a couple of days. Then toss up a quick word to Jesus, asking that he share his peace with you. That you feel his peace directly.

Know this. The Roman Road leads to Jesus, and the two promises from the previous lesson and to the fulfillment of the two promises from the previous lesson, life everlasting and a peace that passes understanding.

LESSON 4

My Addiction: Can the Bible Help?

Not all of my rouge warriors were addicted but some were. Addiction can happen at virtually any age, and it might be involvement with alcohol, prescription or controlled drugs, meth, pills, or sexual addiction. Regardless, God's Word offers help to break free from an addiction. Many former addicts have stated that their involvement with God's Holy Word helped them, giving them strength. Is that just *BS*? Is such help real?

Here are some verses in the Bible that seem to help. At least other addicts have said these helped a bit. Some give warnings as to why you should abstain from certain things while other verses give encouragement that an addiction can be overcome. Pick the verses that speak to you, and then try to figure out why. I guarantee you will learn something about yourself!

Is Addiction Cool?

This sounds like a really dumb question to anyone fighting an addiction, but consider modern advertising. Modern advertising often suggests addictions are cool—stylish men drinking the perfect scotch or women looking cool smoking. We can fight that subtle pressure by becoming aware of it, but the ads are so frequent and overwhelming it can be difficult. Rather than looking to culture, however, we might ask, what does the Bible say?

> Wine is a mocker, strong drink is raging: and whosoever is deceived thereby is not wise (Proverbs 20:1).

> Woe unto them that rise up early in the morning,
> that they may follow strong drink; that continue
> until night, till wine inflame them (Isaiah 5:11)!

These verses tell us how others see us when we are wasted. Sometimes we feel more *cool* or *with it* while being high, but others might just see us as idiots and even worse—losers. So have you ever made an ass out of yourself when high? Hasn't every addict? Hasn't every broken person?

How Should Addicts Respond When Confronted with Drugs?

Interestingly, on the question of how we should respond, the Bible says the same thing as NA and AA. Get out!

> Flee fornication. Many sins that a man does is
> without the body; but he that commits fornication
> sins against his own body (1 Corinthians 6:18).

> For the grace of God that bringeth salvation hath
> appeared to all men, Teaching us that, denying
> ungodliness and worldly lusts, we should live soberly,
> righteously, and godly, in this present world; Looking
> for that blessed hope, and the glorious appearing of
> the great God and our Saviour Jesus Christ; Who
> gave himself for us, that he might redeem us from
> all iniquity (Titus 2:11–14).

Do we escape when its necessary? Do we call our sponsor? Do we seek another social encounter with someone who is not using? If not, we will fall back. Guaranteed!

Will God Help Me?

Okay. You've been reading for a while now. You have to be searching for some help somewhere, so asking if God will help seems reasonable. Even if you've never believed in God, you might want to try now. Many addicts have said that God changed their lives once they've chosen to believe. They can't all be idiots, can they? Why not try God when nothing else has worked?

Here are some verses that might help.

> There hath no temptation taken you but such as is common to man: but God is faithful, who will not suffer you to be tempted above that ye are able; but will with the temptation also make a way to escape, that ye may be able to bear it (1 Corinthians 10:13).

> Blessed is the man that endureth temptation: for when he is tried, he shall receive the crown of life, which the Lord hath promised to them that love him. Let no man say when he is tempted, I am tempted of God: for God cannot be tempted with evil, neither tempteth he any man: But every man is tempted, when he is drawn away of his own lust, and enticed. Then when lust hath conceived, it bringeth forth sin: and sin, when it is finished, bringeth forth death (James 1:12–15).

Sounds like the NA and AA discussions, doesn't it? Addiction leading to death. Well, if so, it might be because it's true. Still, these passages show that God's Word promises his help for those suffering from addiction. Help may come from a deep sense of the wrongness of our actions or in the form of a call to one's sponsor. Maybe you just need to pray.

Sometimes some of the mundane things of life help: getting a job or finding something to do to support the costs of one's halfway house. Any job will sometimes take your mind off the need to get high—cleaning gutters, raking the yard, and cooking for others can all help.

At the very least, doing something along those lines may help you structure your time, and thus, prevent you from thinking about one's addictive desires every single second!

God Will Help Change Your Life

> And be not drunk with wine, wherein is excess; but be filled with the Spirit. Speaking to yourselves in psalms and hymns and spiritual songs, singing and making melody in your heart to the Lord; Giving

thanks always for all things unto God and the Father in the name of our Lord Jesus Christ (Ephesians 5:18– 20).

Therefore if any man be in Christ, he is a new creature: old things are passed away; behold, all things are become new (2 Corinthians 5:17).

In these verses, God is explicitly saying he will help. In fact, going to church is one way to strengthen your relationship with God, bring meaning into your life, and structure your time without getting high (that's the meaning of the speaking/singing hymns and spiritual songs statement above). And don't overlook that last promise: God will make you a new creation—a whole new person—independent of your addiction. He will rebuild your life.

Summary

Repeatedly, the Bible promises that we are new creation in Jesus. There is, perhaps, no more solid help for an addict than the belief that their life be different and that there is sunshine and joy and love in their future. You can find those things in your life if you seek Jesus. In fact, many addicts just like you already have. Now again, send a few words in Jesus's direction. I'm sure God wants a chance to chat with you again.

LESSON 5

Child Sexual Abuse in the Bible

Several of my Rogue Warriors had experienced sexual abuse as a child, both men and women. This lesson had to be in here!

How Frequent Is Child Sexual Abuse?

Child sexual abuse or child molestation is a form of child abuse in which an adult or older adolescent uses a child for sexual stimulation. Forms of child sexual abuse include engaging in sexual activities with a child (whether by asking or pressuring or by other means), indecent exposure (of the genitals, female nipples, etc.), child grooming, or using a child to produce child pornography.

Child sexual abuse can occur in a variety of settings including home, school, or work (in places where child labor is common). Child marriage is one of the main forms of child sexual abuse; UNICEF has stated that child marriage "represents perhaps the most prevalent form of sexual abuse and exploitation of girls." The effects of child sexual abuse can include depression, post-traumatic stress disorder, anxiety, complex stress disorders, propensity to further victimization in adulthood, and physical injury to the child, among other problems. Sexual abuse by a family member is a form of incest and can result in more serious and long-term psychological trauma, especially in the case of parental incest.

The global prevalence of child sexual abuse has been estimated at 19.7 percent for females and 7.9 percent for males. Most sexual abuse offenders are acquainted with their victims approximately thirty percent are relatives of the child, most often brothers, fathers, uncles, or cousins. Around sixty percent are other acquaintances such as *friends* of the family, babysitters, or neighbors. Strangers are the offenders in approximately ten percent of child sexual abuse cases. Most child sexual abuse is committed by men. Studies on female child molesters show that women commit fourteen percent to forty percent of offenses reported against boys and six percent of offenses reported against girls.

Amnon and Tamar: A Bible Story on Sexual Abuse

Sexual abuse has been a plague on society for thousands of years. Even the Old Testament of the Bible contains tragic stories of sexual abuse, rape, and incest. In 2 Samuel, Scriptures tell us that Amnon, the son of David, contrived to get his half sister, Tamar, alone and have sex with her. See 2 Samuel 13:11–12,14, and 20.

> But when she brought them near him to eat, he took hold of her, and said to her, 'Come, lie with me, my sister.' She answered him, 'No, my brother, do not force me; for such a thing is not done in Israel; do not do anything so vile!…But he would not listen to her; and being stronger than she was, he forced her and lay with her…Her brother Absalom said to her, 'Has Amnon your brother been with you? Be quiet for now, my sister; he is your brother; do not take this to heart.' So Tamar remained, a desolate woman, in her brother Absalom's house.

Even in those ancient days, victims were told to keep the abuse a secret. Interestingly enough, Scripture continues to talk about the brothers, the father, and the consequences for them but not much more is said of Tamar. Scripture simply tells us that she remained desolate in her brother's house. She is locked in the silence, shame, violation, and trauma of the abuse she suffered at the hands of her half brother, but the story of destruction that came from this incestuous sexual abuse does not end here.

See 2 Samuel 13:21–33. In this passage, Absolom killed Amnon for his rape of his sister. Still, Absolom had to flee since he'd killed a son of the king. In this story, Amnon pays the price for abuse with his death, but others in the family suffer also because of this abuse. Absolom exacted revenge, and that destroyed him as well.

Take My Daughters! Another Bible Story of Abuse in Genesis 19

Lot is a righteous man, apparently the only righteous man living in the evil city Sodom. When two beautiful angels come to stay as his guests, the men of the city surround the house, demanding the opportunity to rape the angels. They want to abuse the angels sexually! Strangely enough, to fulfill his obligations as a host, Lot offers them an alternative:

> Look, I have two daughters who have not known a man; let me bring them out to you, and do to them as you please; only do nothing to these men, for they have come under the shelter of my roof (Genesis 19:8).

The men objected and demanded the angels, but Lot and his daughters were saved by the angels. However, the town of Sodom paid the price for this sin and was destroyed by God (Genesis 19:9–28). This story suggests several things. First that the entire town paid the price for this sin when it was destroyed. The range of destruction resulting from any sin can be gigantic!

However, there is a subtler message here also, and that is the value of the love of God. The angels in this story represent God's blessings and love for Lot. And while no one suggests that fathers should give their daughters over to sexual abuse, the fact that Lot saw the angels as the cherished blessing of God, he was willing to sacrifice his own daughters to preserve those blessings.

This potential sacrifice for those messengers from God says something about what our highest priority must be—our relationship with the Almighty must supersede any and all earthly concerns!

To push this concept a bit further, for those who have been sexually abused, this suggests that your relationship with the Lord God Almighty is much more critical to who you are than your experience of sexual abuse. For Christians, our earthly experiences do not and should not define us—rather our definition, our worth, and our value is in our relationship with Almighty God. Knowing this can help, at least a bit, with the pain of having been abused.

What Does the Bible Say about Sexual Abuse against Children?

Caring for children appropriately is spoken of highly in the Bible. For example, James 1:27 says that caring for children in need pleases God. "Religion that God our Father accepts as pure and faultless is this: to look after orphans and widows in their distress and to keep oneself from being polluted by the world."

Ephesians 6:4 says, "Fathers, do not exasperate your children; instead, bring them up in the training and instruction of the Lord."

Followers of Jesus are consistently called to love others. Molesting a child can in no way be mistaken for love. Also, the Bible speaks strongly against sexual sin. Sex is a gift given by God meant for marriage, and in the Bible, sexual perversion of any kind is soundly condemned.

How Can I Heal from Being Sexually Abused?

There is hope and healing for all in Jesus Christ even for those who have been sexually abused as children. The journey to healing will look different for each person. It begins with a recognition of the abuse and the damage it has done.

Healing continues as the abused person learns to trust Jesus and release the pain to him. The road is long and will require safe companions such as a counselor, a pastor, and loving family members. However, our Savior, Jesus, said that he is the fulfillment of this prophecy:

> The Spirit of the Lord is on me, because he has anointed me to proclaim good news to the poor. He has sent me to proclaim freedom for the prisoners and recovery of sight for the blind, to set the oppressed free, to proclaim the year of the Lord's favor (Luke 4:18–19).

The Old Testament also offers hope for all the oppressed.

The spirit of the Lord God is upon me, because the Lord has anointed me; he has sent me to bring good news to the oppressed, to bind up the broken-hearted, to proclaim liberty to the captives, and release to the prisoners...to provide for those who mourn in Zion—

to give them a garland instead of ashes, the oil of gladness instead of mourning, the mantle of praise instead of a faint spirit. They will be called oaks of righteousness, the planting of the Lord, to display his glory (Isaiah 61:1,3).

These words of hope from the Old and the New Testament bring freedom to prisoners including those imprisoned by past abuse. In our faith in Jesus, gladness will replace mourning and depression.

Summary

God's Word is clear. Our early life experiences—even something as devastating as childhood sexual abuse—do not have to define us or be a source of pain for all our lives. Our relationship with Jesus defines us, and from that, we take our strength. In becoming a new creation in Jesus, we can and should rise above our past, leaving it behind as we move daily toward the love of God. Jesus makes all things new, and that makes past circumstances irrelevant.

LESSON 6

Homosexuality: Am I Damned by God for All Time?

Over the last couple of years, I've encountered several gay people who were broken, in some degree of pain, and were actively seeking a spiritual dimension in their life. However, as soon as I mentioned Jesus, they shut down the discussion. They had been told clearly (by some Christians among others) that homosexuality or bisexuality was a sin punishable by death. One even quoted Leviticus 18:22 for me.

> You shall not lie with a male as one lies with a female;
> it is an abomination.

Then there is Leviticus 20:12.

> If a man has sexual relations with a man as one does
> with a woman, both of them have done what is
> detestable. They are to be put to death; their blood
> will be on their own heads.

Of course, other nearby passages forbid sleeping with your daughter-in-law, your mother-in-law, your step mom, and your mom. Beasts of the field are covered in there too somewhere, so from these passages, it seems clear that Christianity and an LGBT lifestyle are incompatible. One of my rogue warriors jokingly pointed out that God doesn't like kinky sex at all!

For some in the LGBT community, this abomination clause is a harsh dictum and means they can never be a Jesus follower. They simply refuse to follow any God that denies them what they truly believe is their own sense of self. Some Christians feel the argument on homosexuality of LGBT lifestyles begins and ends here.

Alternatively, in this ongoing debate, some scholars argue about the translations and/or interpretations of these Leviticus passages. There are arguments about what these passages really mean based on translations and interpretation. Here's a couple of examples I pulled off the internet.

The term abomination in modern usage is different than the way in which it was used six thousand years ago or even six hundred years ago for that matter! In the Hebrew Scriptures, an abomination was something that defied a health code. A large portion of the Hebrew Scriptures were based on health codes. So certain codes of hygiene were developed and were seen as very important to follow to the exact degree. If broken, it was actually seen as a betrayal of your community, even immoral! Homosexuality, because of lack of knowledge and understanding, was categorized as unclean, and thus, a break of one of the health codes, thus, an abomination. However, eating shell fish, wearing fabric made of two different types of material, or eating meat and dairy in the same sitting were also considered *abominations*. Most of these codes are not followed today because we recognize that they are simply health codes that existed for a specific community for a specific time. (www.answers.com/Q/Is_homosexuality_an_abomination. Accessed May 23, 2018.)

Homosexuality is abomination. The Christian Right says so all the time, and nonreligious LGBT activists say it too to relegate religion to humanity's dustheap. After all, isn't that what it says in the Bible?

No—and progressive religionists should not use the word. It's a mistranslation and a misconception doing harm to LGBT people and religious people alike.

The word *abomination* is found, of course, in the King James translation of Leviticus 18:22, a translation which reads, "Thou shalt not lie with mankind, as with womankind: it [is] abomination." Yet this is a thoroughly misleading rendition of the word *toevah*, which, while we may not know exactly what it means, definitely does not mean *abomination*. An *abomination* conjures up images of things which should not exist on the face of the earth: three-legged babies, oceans choked with oil, or Cheez-Whiz. And indeed, this is how many religious people regard gays and lesbians. It's Adam and Eve, not Adam and Steve. Homosexuality is unnatural, a perversion, a disease, an abomination.

Yet a close reading of the term *toevah* suggests an entirely different meaning: something permitted to one group and forbidden to another.

Though there is (probably) no etymological relationship, *toevah* basically means taboo. The term *toevah* occurs 103 times in the Hebrew Bible and almost always has the connotation of a non-Israelite cultic practice. In the Torah, the primary *toevah* is foreign forms of worship. The Israelites are instructed not to commit *toevah* because other nations do so. (See Deuteronomy 18:9–12.)(Michaelson, Jay. "Does the Bible Really Call Homosexuality an Abomination?" July 29, 2010.

religiondispatches.org/does-the-bible-really-call-homosexuality-an-abomination. Accessed May 23, 2018.)

*****

Now I'm not an expert on ancient Hebrew, and you probably aren't either, so I'll just let these discussions sit there. Still, I will point out that both of these passages approach the abomination question from the perspective of interpretation of the passage in Leviticus.

Another Option: Does this Ancient Law Apply?

I want to do something different from translation or interpretation arguments (and this is probably me going rogue again). I think I want to ignore that passage altogether! Now I realize how many people I just offended by saying that anything from the Bible should be ignored. The Bible is the Holy Word of God (a principle which I believe), and therefore, must be seen as *infallible* and literal (which is a principle I don't agree with). Of course, here I'm going rogue again, but just stay with me a bit.

The first author above was right in that almost everybody ignores many things in the Bible such as wearing different types of fabric in the same clothing item or the ancient Jewish dietary restrictions. Personally, I love breakfast, so I have bacon all the time along with milk (meat and dairy—an abomination). I also wear cotton underwear and, on occasion, a silk tie! These things place me firmly in the abomination category. With that said, I believe that this ancient dietary dictum, while probably a good principle in the days prior to refrigeration, can be ignored today. I'll bet you ignore it too. Almost all Christians do.

So here's a question. How can we ignore one dictate from the Scriptures (dietary law or clothing taboos) and then tell others they have no right to ignore another dictate on homosexuality? Am I to assume that everyone who is calling homosexual behavior an abomination based on Leviticus is in fact living by the ancient Jewish dietary laws and dress codes found in Leviticus? If not, then get out of my face. They are hypocrites!

The Jerusalem Council

In fact, rather than even suggesting ignoring the Bible, some folks may choose to believe that ancient dictates have been superseded with Jesus's new covenant. In fact, Jesus is a new covenant—an entirely new arrangement. He's the original *new deal!* Thus, to get a better handle on the concept of these Bible dictates that might have been superseded, let's take a look at others who recommended the same concept.

Now we're in some very good company at this point. Some of the folks who actually knew Jesus in life, including a couple of original apostles, have indeed argued that the new covenant of faith in Jesus replaces old, outdated laws and dictates—or at least some of them. The folks making the decision to ignore some Jewish laws were none other than the leaders of the Christian movement in the first century—Peter, Paul, and James, the brothers of Jesus! This is high company indeed!

As a backdrop for this discussion, you should read Acts:10 and 11, and also Acts 15. Those chapters tell about Peter baptizing a Roman soldier, perhaps the first nonJew to join the Jesus followers and also about Peter's vision from God in which God stated that nothing he made should be seen as unclean. The Jerusalem Council itself is discussed in Acts 15.

Now let me set the scene a bit here. Many early Christians believed that all of the followers of Jesus had to be Jewish in every way. Clearly, Jesus was a Jew who followed the ancient laws (most of the time), and all the disciples and early Christians in and around Jerusalem were Jews. In fact, Jesus himself preached mainly to Jews.

Thus, they made the assumption that Jesus's followers had to follow Jewish law including the dietary laws, laws on dress, and the big one—the law that all Jewish male babies had to be circumcised.

Now Peter had gone on an early missionary trip and had been baptizing uncircumcised Greeks and even Romans into Jesus's church (Acts 10 and 11). These guys were not circumcised and given the Greek and Roman cultural celebration of the human form, they were not inclined as adult males to undergo that ritual. I can't say as I blame them. Further, Peter had experienced a dream of vision from God telling him that nothing God made was unclean. In that dream, God specifically told Peter to eat things forbidden by Jewish laws! That's the vision Peter discussed when he was challenged about baptizing men who were not Jewish.

Just a bit later, Paul did the same thing on a missionary trip—baptized uncircumcised men as Jesus followers. Still, the conservative Jews in Jerusalem church heard of this and called Peter and Paul to account before a meeting of early church leaders. This meeting became known as the Jerusalem Council.

Must have been quite a meeting too! Imagine Paul, Peter, James the Just—the brother of Jesus, and other important leaders in the same room lovingly discussing a difference in opinion. Well, like most councils, they discussed the matter and heard from everyone. And James the Just rendered the final verdict on the question: could uncircumcised men become Jesus followers?

Now we must realize that James was leading the Jerusalem church at that time, and as the brother of Jesus, his word commanded respect! His decision is found in Acts 15:19–21. In short, he determined that all Jesus followers should follow certain Jewish dietary laws and several fairly minor ones. But these nonJews could be baptized even if they didn't follow the other laws and that included circumcision!

This decision documents that the Jerusalem Council decided that parts of the Jewish Scriptures could be set aside. More specifically, this decision suggested that the new covenant in Jesus made the ancient law less binding, though not altogether unimportant.

Based on this, is it unreasonable to suggest that homosexual abomination clause (Leviticus 18:22) should simply be set aside? Like many of the Jewish dietary laws or the circumcision mandate, might we consider this abomination clause out-of-date?

Modern understandings in psychology and human sexuality seem to indicate that there is no psychological reason to believe that LGTB behaviors are unhealthy in any way. Given that, we might ask, who are we to damn all such folks to hell? Further, it is widely accepted in the field of psychology today that homosexuality is a reality for many men and women and not merely a *lifestyle choice* as some suggest.

Now Let's Consider the Real Authority

But for Christians, even the hallowed names those men at the Jerusalem Council—James the Just, Peter, and Paul—are not the ultimate authority. Jesus is our authority! So one might well ask, do we see Jesus overturning, amending, or ignoring ancient Jewish law? Certainly, a Rabbi like Jesus could never do that!

On the other hand, Jesus broke almost every expectation of those who followed him! The famous story in John 8:1–11 shows that he did override the law when necessary. We talked about this in the first lesson too because this story is so fundamental to who Jesus was—a man ruled by love and compassion.

In that passage from John, when the Jewish authorities were going to stone an adulterous woman to death, they asked Jesus what he would do. Now understand, the woman was guilty, and ancient Jewish law stated clearly she should be stoned to death. Jesus as a learned Rabbi certainly knew this. However, Jesus found a way to show love and compassion using a question that forced those men to examine themselves. Who is free enough from sin to pass any condemnation? Jesus's words echo through time.

Let he who is without sin, cast the first stone.

In this passage, it is clear that the new covenant of faith in Jesus is that we follow him while he owns the burden for our sin, which indeed override ancient law sometimes. For Christians, Jesus's very presence—his examples of love and caring—are now the law and must supersede harsh judgments.

In fact, for a Christ follower, the love and compassion of Jesus must rule all decisions and all actions. He showed his love and compassion in all he did even to the extent of praying for forgiveness for those who were literally nailing him to a cross and torturing him to death.

> Father forgive them. For they know not what they
> do (Luke 23:34).

His love and compassion were absolute! His example is absolute! That love and compassion must rule in our lives on every question as it did for Jesus.

Summary

So for now I'll move a bit back from my rogue statement that we should ignore any part of the Bible. The Bible is God's Holy Word and cannot ever be ignored. Yet I will stand and die on the idea that Jesus's love and compassion for all must govern all our decisions as Christ followers. That amazing love and compassion forces all Christians, I think, to love and accept all others into our body as fellow believers without holding up the impediment of dated practices of ancient Jewish law. Neither circumcision or the abomination clause should prevent anyone from knowing Jesus.

In this, I stand with Paul, Peter, and James the Just as well as Jesus. If we have accepted Jesus, we are truly blessed members of his followers and will be destined to live with him through all eternity—circumcised or not and gay or not.

Lesson 7

Dealing with My Anger

Sometimes persons with challenged backgrounds—perhaps a troubled childhood or a recent divorce or breakup—seem to be unusually angry. Many things can make us angry, and all of us get angry at times. We might get angry when someone insults us or when we feel judged by others. Maybe we feel someone has been unfair to us. We might get angry when we realize we are alone in the world while others seem to have someone in their lives, or we might covet the *ease* of someone's life.

We might even get angry when someone tries to help us, or we might be angry at ourselves for our bad decisions. That was and is the case with some of my Rogue Warriors: they frequently get very angry when I try to help them simply because they were forced in those times to admit to themselves they needed some help!

In fact, for many of the folks I've worked with, anger is a huge issue. It is no accident that almost all men and women in halfway houses and drug court have to take anger management classes.

So what can we do when feeling angry? First let's look at the psychology of anger and then at what can the Bible teach us about anger.

The Psychology of Anger: Where Does Anger Come from?

Does your anger sometimes seem to come up within you out of nowhere? Do you sometimes find yourself enraged over small things? Are you sometimes angry at nothing at all? Do you *lose it* sometimes and then feel like you should apologize for a comment you made while you were angry?

Psychology has long postulated that anger, like most emotions, can be caused by simple events. But it then frequently seems to grow within our minds, becoming greater even though one has left the situation that originally produced the anger. Further, situations that we perceive to be similar to the circumstances that originally produced anger within us can trigger the same anger and rage which resulted from the earlier event. This is sometimes referred to as displaced anger since the anger really comes from an earlier occurrence but is put on display after a later different event.

Finally, psychologists tell us that anger can *grow*. Over time, we can actually get angrier just by thinking about a previous event or previous comment from someone.

In this way, anger can become overbearing and all consuming. It might then *boil over* and erupt into hateful and/or highly destructive actions. Those who have good cause to be angry (victims of abuse for example who might have been forced to contain their anger and rage initially) might become very explosive at a much later time. Thus, women or men who were abused as children might find that even the smallest thing in their adulthood perhaps a circumstance similar to one in their childhood might produce an overwhelming rage.

How Should Christ Followers Deal with Anger?

The Bible does provide lessons on anger, and we're getting to some below. However, first we need to discuss a biblical concept. *Apostolic authority* was a concept developed by leaders in the church in the early first and second centuries. To have apostolic authority meant that you either knew Jesus before the resurrection and perhaps followed him in his earthy ministry or came to know him soon after the resurrection. Thus, all of the original twelve disciples, and perhaps Mary Magdalene, would be considered the *true* or most sound *authorities* on Jesus, his life, and his teachings. In fact, the words and guidance of Peter for example, a man who was an original disciple, meant more to the early Christians than the words of such important figures as Martin Luther or even Billy Graham.

In terms of apostolic authority, one unique writer among the many men who wrote the Bible is James. He was the half brother of Jesus, so while he was not an original follower of Jesus—not one of the original twelve disciples—he was considered to have great apostolic authority. Like Paul, James soon became a follower of Jesus after the resurrection and then became the leader of the Christian community in Jerusalem.

For this reason, the letter of James, one of only two letters in the Bible written by a relative of Jesus (the other is Jude), is considered an important statement of what it means to be Christian—a statement based on great apostolic authority. This letter assumes that the readers are followers of Jesus and already know the story of Jesus, so the letter focuses on how to live as Christians. Lucky for us, this letter includes instructions on dealing with anger, instructions from a man who actually knew Jesus! Here's what James had to say on anger.

> What causes fights and quarrels among you? Don't
> they come from your desires that battle within you?
> You desire but do not have, so you kill. You covet
> but you cannot get what you want, so you quarrel
> and fight. You do not have because you do not ask
> God (James 4: 1–2).

What does this section from James tell us about anger? What does *battle within you* mean in this context? Could this be a Bible version of displaced anger?

It is amazing to me, a man who knows both psychology and the Scriptures, that parallels like this exist everywhere in the Bible. Here, James is saying the same things about anger as modern psychology—that it comes from within us and is often displaced. Our anger is related to many events and circumstances that happened long ago! It is almost as if anger moves from one event to another, and James, the brother of Jesus, knew this 2000 years ago! He was a wise man indeed.

Anger Leads to Sin

So what else can we learn about anger from the Bible? Here's a lesson from Paul.

In your anger do not sin. Do not let the sun go down while you are still angry, and do not give the devil a foothold. Anyone who has been stealing must steal no longer, but must work, doing something useful with their own hands, that they may have something to share with those in need. Do not let any unwholesome talk come out of your mouths, but only what is helpful for building others up according to their needs, that it may benefit those who listen (Ephesians 4: 26–29).

What is the danger that Paul speaks of with anger? His concern is that anger makes us sin. Is that valid? Do we do sin when angry? Do we do dumb, destructive things to others when we are angry? Do our words become cruel? Do we overstate our point rather than listen to the points of others?

Finally, how do we live up to the standard "do not let the sun go down while you are angry?" Would our lives be better if we did?

Is Anger Ever Good?

Get rid of all bitterness, rage and anger, brawling and slander, along with every form of malice (Ephesians 4: 31).

My dear brothers and sisters, take note of this: Everyone should be quick to listen, slow to speak and slow to become angry, because human anger does not produce the righteousness that God desires (James 1: 19–20).

What do these verses tell us? Doesn't this last verse seem to prohibit human anger? The phrase *slow to become angry* seems to suggest that we will all feel anger, but in Ephesians, Paul says to get rid of all bitterness and rage.

What Should We Do about Anger?

So these verses do give guidance on how we deal with anger. They do provide some things to do, and of course, a chat with God is always warranted. Here's a list of ideas to deal with anger.

Pray: When you want to say something cruel to someone, take a quick quite breath and whisper to yourself, "God give me help here, please!" Perhaps you can then talk about the anger rather than actually express it!

Listen: We should listen more carefully to others. Maybe we misunderstood them, and there is no reason to be angry. We can also *talk it out* with them. As the passage says, do not let the sun go down…

Guard our thoughts: We must learn that we control our thoughts. We can actually say to ourselves, "I won't allow that thought. I'll find another thought." We can, thus, get rid of much of our anger just by deciding not to be angry. We can, with practice, develop fairly extensive control over all thoughts including angry thoughts. This is what Christians are instructed to do. In fact, that's called maturity.

Watch our words: Like our thoughts, we have to learn to *watch* our words. We have the responsibility as mature men and women to be careful and considerate of what we say and how we say it.

This is one area in which modern psychology and the Bible agree completely. Anger is our emotion, and we can learn to be in control of it with practice.

Summary

Anger is felt by everyone for a vast array of reasons. Some anger comes from our own bad decisions, and other anger seems justified because of how we may have been treated. Many times, our expressions of anger are displaced anger and are really related to previous events in our lives. However, the Bible is clear that anger usually is very destructive and warns humans to get rid of anger they feel. In fact, the Bible sections on anger agree with modern understandings in psychology that *battles within ourselves* can be highly destructive when those battles lead to anger in other situations. In short, we should strive to pray about anger, listen more carefully to others, talk about our anger, and guard our thoughts and our words if we are to live as Jesus did.

Lesson 8

Dealing with Disappointment

Disappointment can happen at any time, but seems to happen more around Holiday seasons such as Christmas. This season can be very hard on addicts and persons with challenged family backgrounds. It is an emotional time anyway for many people, and at times, it can involve some disappointment. Some folks have memories of Christmases past that were less than pleasant. Maybe your family let you down at some point or abandoned you altogether. Maybe for some of us, our own bad choices put us in a place where a family relationship was impossible.

Still, for most people, broken or not, feeling some disappointment at any holiday season is not unusual.

My mom was a loving woman who was the center of our Christmas. She played the piano when we sang carols as a family, and we always gathered at her house for the season. She loved the season and loved her family. She often had an emotional high on the holidays. However, as soon as they were over, she always had a fairly large emotional letdown. She used to say that all her *kids* were grown and living somewhere else and that when we left, she got depressed. Toward Christmas Eve when the family got together, it was sometimes like walking on eggshells, trying not to mention the fact that on Christmas Day, we all disappeared. And she would get depressed.

Whether depression results from a holiday season or not, it is still quite difficult to deal with. In almost every case, the halfway house men or the other broken men and women I've worked with experienced some level of depression. In some cases, the depression was so overwhelming that it blotted out all other emotion. It's almost like the blackest cloud can blot out the sun.

Bible Responses to Disappointment

So what does the Bible say for those who are disappointed or deep into depression? Here are a few verses that have, for others, brought some degree of hope.

I lift up my eyes to the hills. From where does my help come? My help comes from the Lord, who made heaven and earth. He will not let your foot be moved; he who keeps you will not slumber. Behold, he who keeps Israel will neither slumber nor sleep. The Lord is your keeper; the Lord is your shade on your right hand (Psalm 121: 1–8).

This was, in our family, a source of strength for many generations. When I read this, it brings some measure of peace into my heart. Here are several other verses that have helped others combat depression.

Do not be anxious about anything, but in everything by prayer and supplication with thanksgiving let your requests be made known to God. And the peace of God, which surpasses all understanding, will guard your hearts and your minds in Christ Jesus (Philippians 4: 6–7).

What does Paul tell us in Philippians above? His suggestion for when one feels depressed is to take the matter up with God through prayer. Of course, that is quite meaningless, unless one has a foundation of belief in God and a habit of frequent prayer. This is why it is so important to build a relationship with God through Jesus by chatting with him several times each day. Here's another verse that can guide us.

> "And we know that for those who love God all
> things work together for good, for those who are
> called according to his purpose" (Romans 8:28).

Paul again is the author here, but his message is somewhat broader. Here, he states that even when we are depressed about a particular situation or circumstance, we simply have to trust God and believe in his larger plan for us even though we might not know what that plan is. That is very hard to do even for Christians with a practice of faith over many years, and it is nearly impossible for a new believer to trust God that much. Still, to attain God's peace—the peace that passes understanding—this level of trust must be our goal. James, the brother of Jesus, likewise spoke of trusting God's overall plan.

> For I know the plans I have for you, declares the
> Lord, plans for welfare and not for evil, to give you
> a future and a hope (Jeremiah 29:11).

I'm Disappointed When God's Plan Holds Bad Things

Of course, even if we trust God and his plan, that does not mean that bad things won't happen. Sometimes our fears are well founded (e.g. I might be sentenced to jail, my spouse might file for divorce, or this cancer might kill me or my child). While God promises us help and comfort, he does not promise us that all things will work out as we want. Sometimes persons pray and pray, and horrible things happen anyway.

Here is an extreme example. Consider the early Christians during the period in which Rome was persecuting all Jesus followers (AD 80 until AD 300). Those followers of Jesus were being led into the coliseum where they would be torn apart by lions or other beasts. In ancient Rome, this provided a spectator sport for the Roman citizens. We know that those Christians often prayed to God to be saved from that horrible death. Of course, in the Old Testament, there is the example of Daniel who was fed to hungry lions but survived the lion's den without being attacked. God protected Daniel! However, we also know that most of those Christians during the persecution period, once they were in the coliseum, didn't survive. They died in great pain.

Now how can anyone say that is God's plan? How disappointed will you be if you earnestly pray for God to deliver you from a bad situation and the horrible event happens anyway? Do we then just assume that God is the most evil being in the universe?

Again, the Bible provides help. In fact, we have Jesus's own assurance to a man who was being tortured to death on a cross.

> Jesus answered him, "Truly I tell you, today you will be with me
> in paradise" (Luke 23: 43).

Of course, this is what Jesus said to the robber who was being crucified right beside Jesus himself. In this example, Jesus doesn't promise the man he will alleviate the man's pain. He doesn't promise the man will be saved from death. What he does promise is the immanent, indeed the immediate, experience of God's glory in heaven. Note the exact promise of Jesus. "Today, you will be with me in paradise."

Now let's return and look at this from the perspective of those Christians in the coliseum. Imagine you, your wife or husband, and children are herded into that arena with fifteen other Christians and a few criminals. Here come the lions. The humans gather in a small bunch—some protection in numbers for a few seconds. You might try to position yourself between your children and the hungry beasts. Then a lion you didn't see takes your youngest daughter by the arm and pulls her out of the pack. Several others pounce on that child and begin to feed. You hear the screams and still have to fight off the other lions which you do for just a moment or two more, but then one has your arm, pulling you away as others pounce on your legs, groin, and rip out your stomach. You are about to die while still listening to the screams of your children.

Of course, I'm intentionally making it as horrible as possible in order to make a point. Still, it occurs to me that many of my friends, these broken people—in fact, most of my Rogue Warriors—have experienced things exactly this horrible!

Anyway here's the point. While horrible things happen, even if we should experience the most horrid torture and death imaginable, I truly believe that we can, in that last instance of life, experience God's compassion. Personally, I imagine that when that horrible moment of death comes—when I'm eaten by lions or more likely in today's world, cancer— just as my eyes close and my mind dims for the final time on this earth, I will suddenly sense my eyes opening and will then see the face of God. It is just as Jesus promised in the passage above—an immediate experience of God's glory! "Today, you will be with me in paradise." This concept is likewise suggested by other Bible verses.

I have said these things to you, that in me you may have peace. In the world you will have tribulation. But take heart; I have overcome the world (John 16:33).

Whatever you do, work heartily, as for the Lord and not for men, knowing that from the Lord you will receive the inheritance as your reward. You are serving the Lord Christ (Colossians 3: 23– 25).

In these verses, God does not promise the removal of pain, death, or disappointment for his Jesus followers. He promises us the greatest gift of all, his presence.

So How Then Do We Deal with Disappointment?

The answer here is simple. We build a relationship over time by chatting with God as frequently as possible. Then as disappointment, pain, or horrible events come, we will be prepared to deal with them, knowing that they are a part of God's plan in some way. It really does come down to a matter of trust. We either build a habit of trusting God and his plan or we don't. Those that do experience his peace even during disappointments.

In nothing be anxious, but in everything, by prayer and petition with thanksgiving, let your requests be made known to God. And the peace of God, which surpasses all understanding, will guard your hearts and your thoughts in Christ Jesus (Philippians 4: 6–7).

This must be our goal for ourselves and all Rogue Warriors. Let's all learn to bring our fears, disappointments, and other issues to God, so that we might sense the peace that passes understanding.

Summary

All of us deal with disappointments in life. And sometimes, there can be more disappointment and more stress around the holidays. God's Word indicates that we will be disappointed at times, but that, with prayer and openness to God, we can deal with it. He does not promise us that bad things won't happen but that we will be blessed with his peace in this life or the next if we believe in him. Further, he tells us to bring our disappointments to him through prayer. In prayer, we make our concerns known to God, and this alone will bring us some degree of peace.

More fundamentally, prayer is our way to build a relationship with God. In dealing with disappointments, we can and should pray about it without ceasing. In fact, psychology has long noted the benefits of prayer emotionally. For believers, prayer can bring peace, and the stronger the belief, the more peace it brings.

Lesson 9

Dealing with Frustrations

Life is filled with frustrations, and sometimes they overwhelm us. We work hard, try to spend wisely, and still have bills that we can't pay sometimes. Other times, the person we love that we must depend on lets us down. Husbands or wives sometimes run away. Parents abandon kids or worse, are cruel to them. Sometimes everything in life seems to pile up, and we simply don't know what to do. Emotional paralysis can result, and we sometimes just withdraw from everything. Other times, we lash out at others.

At times, it just seems easier to simply crawl back into a bottle or into a meth habit. Just a few pills ease the tension so nicely, at least for a while. Most of us have used some of these options from time to time, and addicts use this option frequently. Still, anyone honest with themselves will see that these options don't work for long. So how does a Christian respond to these kinds of frustrations or other frustrations? Can we simply ignore them? Can we find help? What can we learn from the Bible?

First Come to God

Come to me, all who labor and are heavy laden, and I will give you rest. Take my yoke upon you, and learn from me, for I am gentle and lowly in heart, and you will find rest for your souls (Matthew 11:28–29).

I have said these things to you, that in me you may have peace. In the world you will have tribulation. But take heart; I have overcome the world (John 16:33).

Do not repay evil with evil or insult with insult. On the contrary, repay evil with blessing, because to this you were called so that you may inherit a blessing. For whoever would love life and see good days must keep their tongue from evil and their lips from deceitful speech. They must turn from evil and do good; they must seek peace and pursue it (I Peter 3: 9–11).

What can we see in these verses? Does God promise us help? Under what conditions? Again, what must we do to have the peace of God even when we are deeply frustrated? How do we get that deep certainty of peace in our hearts? Does such a sense of peace actually help to turn us from evil? One difference between actual believers and those who merely profess faith in Christ is that the actual believers can have the peace of God. Each verse above emphasizes that we must first know God and *come to God*. Simply put, we cannot have the peace of God until we are first at peace with God.

Next, Be Humble and Prayerfully Ask God for Peace

> Humble yourselves, therefore, under the mighty hand of God so that at the proper time he may exalt you, casting all your anxieties on him, because he cares for you (1 Peter 5:6–7).

> But God gives us grace, and scriptures say, God opposes the proud but gives grace to the humble. Therefore submit to God (James 4: 6–7).

Some of us don't do humble very well. That would be me along with most of my Rogue Warriors. Sometimes I feel like my pride or iron will is the only thing I have left, and if I give that up, I lose everything. I'd go so far as to say that few broken people are particularly good at being humble probably because they have faced challenges in life that many others haven't. Pride can be a powerful and effective defense against pain. Nevertheless, God clearly commands us to be humble before him to find his peace in our lives. If we do not have peace that passes understanding in our lives, it is probably fair to say that we should rededicate ourselves to God.

When was the last time each of us got on our knees and prayed earnestly to God that we might dedicate ourselves to him and know his peace?

What Is God's Peace Like?

First God's peace is founded in prayer and reading his Word. The Bible tells us to pray repeatedly and read the Word all the time. If you have a family, read a Bible verse before each prayer at the beginning of the meal. Teach your children God's Word. In the halfway house, read the Bible together and pray together.

Next, God's peace brings unimaginable courage. "Fear not, for I am with you; be not dismayed, for I am your God; I will strengthen you, I will help you, I will uphold you with my righteous right hand" (Isaiah 41:10).

> In nothing be anxious, but in everything, by prayer and petition with thanksgiving, let your requests be made known to God. And the peace of God, which surpasses all understanding, will guard your hearts and your thoughts in Christ Jesus (Philippians 4: 6–7).

Summary

God promises his peace and his support to all who believe in him and follow him. He does not promise an easy life. Rather, he promises that the challenges of life, no matter how daunting, will not overcome us. Still, we must approach God and be humble before him, prayerfully asking for his peace and then receiving his help when it is offered. Our pride must never prevent us from coming to God no matter how much our pride has protected us before. Once we have God's peace, we will see his will for our future. And while it may not be what we planned or it may even be quite dangerous, it will be a peaceful joyous life—safe within God's plan for us.

LESSON 10

Let's Talk Suicide

I talked with several persons last week about getting their lives together and things that have been happening to them, and the topic of suicide came up on three different occasions. Twice I was told that one of those folks had attempted suicide. For broken people, suicide is a topic that demands attention.

In the late 1980s, I had to admit professionally that I was useless when I was asked for help with suicide. It was a national news story, a reported suicide pact where four teenagers committed suicide together. This followed a series of suicides the previous year. The story became known as the Bergenfield Suicide Pact. I was not directly involved, but I taught at Rutgers University in educational psychology, and the local school district reached out to our university department for help. We had little to offer since that was one of the first suicide agreements in history.

Over the next few months, I wrote a couple of research articles on suicide risk factors among students with disabilities and so on. Still, the fact is, I'd been useless to other professionals when there had been a serious need for information. It was not a good feeling.

I did, however, learn a lot! I learned that at that time, there was a *suicide line* or a lower age limit of about fourteen over fifteen years. You had suicides or attempted suicides below that age limit only very rarely but a sharp increase in suicide attempts thereafter. Today that age limit has gone down somewhat, following the age onset of puberty (which has likewise gone down), and if there is a *suicide line*, it is around eleven or twelve today. I also learned the other cold, hard statistics.

Facts on Suicide

Suicide risk factors include mental disorders such as depression, bipolar disorder, schizophrenia, personality disorders, and substance abuse including alcoholism and use of benzodiazepines. Others factors include stress resulting from financial difficulties, troubles with relationships, sexual or physical abuse, or bullying. These are exactly the same risk factors that result in the broken lives of most broken people. Further, those who have attempted suicide are at a much higher risk for future attempts, making broken people a high risk group for suicide.

Common methods to attempt suicide include hanging, poisoning, and firearms. Firearms account for fifty-one percent of suicides in the USA but are used by males more than females.

Suicide is the 10th leading cause of death in the USA and worldwide. Each year, 44,965 Americans die from suicide. Further, there are an estimated ten to twenty million nonfatal attempted suicides every year.

Men die from suicide 3.7 times more frequently than women. However, suicide attempts are more common in females. Also, suicide in the US is still most common among those between fifteen and thirty.

Those are the facts. Much less is known about the feelings, the deep sense of depression, aloneness, fear, or self-loathing that sometimes plays a role in attempted suicide. Why and how do we get to a point where eliminating ourselves seems more reasonable a choice than living? Can a faith in Jesus help?

We Are God's Temple

Do you not know that you are God's temple and that God's Spirit dwells in you? If anyone destroys God's temple, God will destroy him. God's temple is holy, and you are that temple (1 Corinthians 3: 16–17).

This passage from the New Testament tells us that suicide is not an option for a believer. Further, if there is love, concern, and immediate help from an all-powerful, all-knowing God who cares deeply for each of us as individuals, how can one commit suicide?

We Are Not Our Own

You are not your own, for you were bought with a price. So glorify God in your body (1 Corinthians 6:20).

This is another Bible based view also that informs us on the suicide issue. While we have responsibility for ourselves and our actions, we do not own ourselves. We belong to God. Jesus bought and paid for us, and we cannot destroy what belongs to God. Paul even used the concept of slavery when he said he was a slave to the Almighty.

For when you were slaves of sin, you were free in regard to righteousness. Therefore what benefit were you then deriving from the things of which you are now ashamed? For the outcome of those things is death. But now having been freed from sin and enslaved to God, you derive your benefit resulting in sanctification, and the outcome, eternal life (Romans 6: 20– 22).

Crying Out to God

So I say to you: Ask and it will be given to you; seek and you will find; knock and the door will be opened to you (Luke 11:9).

When the righteous cry for help, the Lord hears and delivers them out of all their troubles. The Lord is near to the brokenhearted and saves the crushed in spirit. Many are the afflictions of the righteous, but the Lord delivers him out of them all (Psalm 34: 17–20).

If one even thinks of suicide, they must cry out! This can be done by calling a suicide line, a minister, a church, or simply shouting out to God. Here's an example.

The most impressive *Cry Out to God* story I've heard lately was from a former drug dealer and drug kingpin speaking in a Baptist pulpit in a rural country church. He has to remain nameless for his own safety as explained below. In his former life, he had been a money man for a drug cartel in Nicaragua, South America. He lived the lifestyle you see in movies—all the women he could want and trash bags filled with between twenty-five to fifty million in cash sitting at his apartment, waiting to be *laundered*. He was used to prostitutes between the ages twelve and seventeen, and he often took two or three at a time. After all, the same cartel that sold drugs worldwide also marketed those young girls in that country—most were girls that had no other option to feed themselves. He even had his own bodyguard.

Then one day, someone decided not to trust him anymore. A *hit* was ordered. He learned of the kill order and immediately fled back to the USA with nothing. He felt his life was over, and the life he'd known was indeed over. Several months later, one bleak day with a cheap weapon he'd purchased with his last funds, he was about to kill himself. Then he looked up and saw a church. He figured it couldn't hurt, and he had nothing to lose. He walked in.

As he tells the story, "God saved me that day, and on the next day, God told me what to do." Note the main point here. He cried out to God by merely walking into a church and saying a prayer. He had nothing to lose like most folks contemplating suicide, but he cried out to God. He was saved that day. Such things really do happen from time to time in almost any church. The same thing happens occasionally in a jail cell or a halfway house. Lives can change right there where you are as you read this because God lives there. He lives everywhere and anywhere.

God then told this man, "Go back." So within a few days, he got on a plane and went back to Nicaragua. He was doing what God told him to do. While he didn't feel he could do anything about the drug business, he did feel he might be able to save one or two young girls from the life of prostitution. The kill order was still active, but God told him what to do, and he did it. Once in country, he saw a young prostitute on a corner and simply asked her if she wanted to continue as a prostitute or "Come with me right now to a place where you'll have food and a warm bed and get to go to school." He was talking about a Christian orphanage in another part of the country. She chose to go with him.

The next day, some of the other girls also went with him. Thus, he began doing God's work, rescuing some of these girls from the cartel prostitution business. Now those actions began to cut into the money for the cartel, so another hit was put on him. But he says he was lucky in that the job was actually given to his former bodyguard.

That bodyguard, rather than kill him outright, simply watched him save two or three girls from the street and then approached his target and asked, "What in hell are you doing?" His testimony was shared with his bodyguard who was touched by the story. The bodyguard went back to his bosses and pretended he couldn't find the target. Later, the bodyguard actually joined this changed man in helping rescue young girls.

Most of the time today he spends in the USA seeking funds for his ministry to fight child trafficking in South America. Still, even today, this man returns several times a year to Nicaragua where he, his former bodyguard (and new rescue partner along with one or two others) go on *rescue missions*. The *hit* order is still active, so on the rescue missions, they go armed. Thus, they only allow former police officers or former soldiers to join that rescue band. Still, they pick up young women who want out of the trade and get them into orphanage homes in another part of the country.

This is now known as the Breaking Chains Ministry (breakingchains.org). For interesting reading, look at that website and review the *training* section. While all Christians can contribute to this ministry (money and time for orphanages, etc.), only select individuals with a police or military background are eligible for training for the rescue teams.

Still, don't overlook two points. First calling out to God will change your life particularly if you have nothing else to lose. Next even the most despicable type of person can find salvation in God's house as well as an important mission to do.

Summary

Suicide is not an option for God's people. Because we are God's temple and do not belong to we ourselves, we cannot destroy what is God's. Moreover, when such a black depression does seem to overcome us, crying out to God will save even the most desperate among us. This can include calling a suicide line, walking into a church, talking to a friend, or saying a prayer right where you sit. Reach out to Jesus, and you will find rest.

LESSON 11

Damaged Goods: Am I Worthy of Love?

I Feel Like I'm Worthless! Am I Worthy of Love?

I've had several discussions along these lines with various broken people over the years. I've learned that many individuals with a background of sexual abuse and often other types of abuse as well don't consider themselves worthy of love. They seem to feel, "How could anyone love me?" From a psychological perspective, it is a fact that those who are abused or neglected early in life begin to believe in the perspective of their abusers—that they are unworthy of love. Many persons fighting addictions likewise have a sense that they are all alone in the world—that they cannot be loved because they are unworthy of love.

Because of that deep-seated belief in their own worthlessness, these persons often choose relationships that support that view—that they are worthless. These individuals will choose and hold on for dear life to relationships with abusive persons, believing that such a relationship is all that they deserve. Thus, the cycle of abuse continues.

Some persons with an abusive history sometimes take this feeling of unworthiness even further. They sometimes believe that they are unworthy of not only of the love of any partner but also of God's love. Thus, even though they may believe in God, they might wonder if going to church is worth it. They simply believe they are completely worthless.

So what does the Bible say about our worthiness for love? What messages can we glean from Jesus as to our worthiness?

All Fall Short…

> For all have sinned and fall short of the glory of God
> (Romans 3:23).

We can begin with the famous line from Romans. This line, taken alone, seems to suggest the unworthiness of all of us. In fact, many ministers use this line as the first line in the discussion when they are talking with nonbelievers (The first part of the Roman Road discussed earlier!). Thus, the starting position for Christians is that we are all unworthy of God's love. However, anyone who has ever watched a football game knows that the start off position—two teams facing each other during a kickoff—is not the definition of the game. There is much more to follow, and in fact, the start off position is rarely seen anymore throughout the rest of the game.

Likewise, it is simply foolish to think that the beginning position of salvation is the end of the story.

Paul, in the book of Romans, goes on to say much more just like there is much more to the football game than the starting position. Paul initially reinforces our worthlessness in Romans 6:23 when he says:

> For the wages of sin is death…

Here he means not only death in this life, but also *forever death* or separation from God forever. Surely the forever death—a fading into nothingness, is much worse than merely death. So the initial picture is pretty dreary. Not only are we all worthless but we will face our separation from God forever and ultimately cease to exist.

Then a Reversal of Meaning

Still, Paul quickly changes the discussion—this is the breakout run after the kickoff when a team moves seriously downfield. Paul reverses the meaning by stating at the end of Romans 6:23:

> …but the gift of God is eternal life through Jesus
> Christ our Lord.

Now this is quite a reversal of meaning. We are not worthless. Rather, God has chosen to give us eternal life in him. In fact, Jesus chose you thousands of years before you were even born! Paul continues:

> …But God demonstrates his own love toward us,
> in that while we were yet sinners, Christ died for us
> (Romans 5: 8).

Our sins are now forgiven. Our debt has been paid not only for sins we have already committed but also for sins we have not yet committed! What does this say about our worthiness in God's eyes? Would God sacrifice his son and put his son through torture and death on the cross for unworthy beings? Clearly, the New Testament view is that man is worthy of the most dear, most painful sacrifice God can make—his own son's death paid the price for our behavior.

But we can make this point more demonstrative. Believing we are unworthy is an affront to God! Even if an early history of abuse or emotional neglect in our early life taught us we have no value, believing that belittles Jesus's sacrifice on the cross! Thus, such a belief is an affront—an insult in some sense—to the sacrifice that Jesus made. Jesus did not suffer unimaginable pain and die a horrid death for unworthy beings! Feeling unworthy, in the face of the reality that Jesus gave his life for us, is an insult to that sacrifice! Simply stated, no Christian has the right to believe he or she is unworthy no matter how large his or her burden of sin. Jesus paid our debt specifically because we are worthy!

In fact, we are God's breath—God's expression of his will in this universe! We are, in our very existence, worthy of love and all of the joy that God has promised in the Bible!

Other Lessons from the Bible

> What is man that thou are mindful of him? The son
> of man that thou care for him? You made him a little
> lower than heavenly angels and crowned him with
> glory and honor (Psalms 8:4–5).

What does this psalm say of our worthiness? What is more worthy in God's kingdom than man? Mankind, each of us, is only slightly lower than God and his angles! How then can anyone believe they are unworthy? Even those who are deeply convinced of their own unworthiness are yet worthy, through Jesus' love and sacrifice for us all.

> You yourselves have seen what I did to the Egyptians, and how I bore you on eagles' wings and brought you to myself. Now therefore, if you will indeed obey my voice and keep my covenant, you shall be my treasured possession among all peoples, for all the earth is mine; and you shall be to me a kingdom of priests and a holy nation (Exodus 19:4–6).

What does this say of our worthiness? How can we feel unworthy if God treats us as his treasured possession?

But What Does This Mean to Me?

Is this stuff for real? Is it possible that I am really worthy? That all mankind is worthy? Can this help us, on an individual level, fight the sense that we are unworthy? How do we change our belief that we are not worthy? How can the Bible help us to end the pattern of abusive relationships based on our sense of unworthiness? Two simple answers: prayer and reading!

First pray earnestly and often that God reveal to you his love for you. And through that, his desire for you is to have good, healthy, meaningful relationships that are rich in love and free from abuse.

Next read God's Word. Read and reflect on the passages above when your mood is bleak and the night is closing in. These passages have and will continue to help people through tough times. Indeed, these passages have prevented suicide in the past and will in the future. Simply reading the Bible regularly can and will can change who you are!

Now you're probably thinking, "Get real! Can reading these verses really change our mood, change our mind about our worthiness?

The good news is that reading God's Word does exactly that. This is why God's Word has so much meaning—it can bring peace to us simply by reading certain Scripture. Psalm 23 is a great example of this.

Of course, sometimes Bible lessons seem far removed from our deeper sense of self. Also, simply reading these verses once, even if we believe them, will probably not change our deep sense of worthlessness. It takes many months or years of faith in Jesus to develop the peace he speaks off, but you should start immediately! That is how you get to where you wish to go—a deep sense of your own worthiness!

Perhaps we should end with an assertion that we are most worthy. Indeed, in Jesus, we are conquerors of the world! Let's close by reading Romans 8: 37–39. Then let's ask, "If God is for us, who can be against us?"

Summary

All are worthy in the sight of God. We are made worthy by Jesus's sacrifice. Our fallen relationship with God has been made whole again, and our sins, both in the past and the future, are forgiven. We are worthy of God's love, and if that is true, we must strive to see that we are worthy of love of our children, our spouse, and all others in our world.

LESSON 12

How Guilty Am I?

Many folks with nontraditional backgrounds feel a burden of guilt that is gigantic. Of course, this parallels the previous discussion on being worthy of love and even worthy of God's love. How about you guys? Do you ever ask questions like, "Why did I ruin my marriage? Why did I allow my drug habit to screw up my child? Why did I waste those years of my life?" Such questions represent a self-judgment that is self-condemning, perhaps nearly paralyzing. Such guilt is stress-inducing and can cause us to cut ourselves off from others, except for false, shallow relationships.

This level of guilt leads to empty lives and failed relationships. This can lead us right back to our addictive behavior! Sometimes the guilt is associated with bad choices we've made in our lives, but often, both the guilt and those bad choices are based in traumatic insult or abuse that may have happened to us early in life. Regardless of the cause, it helps us to know that God's Word can help with our guilt.

Bible Lessons on Guilt

> For all have sinned and fall short of the glory of God (Romans 3:23).

> Just so, I tell you, there will be more joy in heaven over one sinner who repents than over ninety-nine righteous persons who need no repentance (Luke 15:7).

What do these verses tell us about guilt? Does God want us to feel guilty? What is guilt and how does it benefit us if it does? Is there such a thing as guilt that is justified? Should we allow ourselves to feel guilty and to be trapped in guilt? Does it perhaps motivate us to do better in our lives?

To get a handle on this, some ministers differentiate between *false guilt* and real guilt. False guilt is a harsh, negative feeling we often have that we associate with our shame for our past misbehaviors. This guilt will sometimes paralyze us and freezes out our emotions. This can kill our relationships with other people. False guilt is also very often associated with harsh judgments from others or worry about how others see us.

Real guilt, on the other hand, is our guilt as perceived by God. Real guilt is a fundamental fact of human existence since Adam. As the Bible says, "All fall short of the glory of God." Real guilt is our falling short of God's desires for us in our lives. Let's explore each.

False Guilt Is Judgment

False guilt is our judgment on we ourselves. Does God want us judging ourselves? Can that be of benefit? What does God say of judgment?

> Judge not, that ye be not judged. For with what judgment ye judge, ye shall be judged (Matthew 7: 1–2).

Does this say, judge not, except for judging ourselves? Does this leave any leeway for judging ourselves? Can we judge ourselves given this Bible instruction?

> Therefore, there is now no condemnation for those who are in Christ Jesus, because through Christ Jesus the law of the Spirit who gives life has set you free from the law of sin and death (Romans 8: 1–2).

The Bible makes clear that judgment of guilt is reserved for God in these passages, and as such, we should not judge ourselves harshly. Now we must honestly evaluate our behavior and pray for God's forgiveness. We should also celebrate our movements forward. Still, we have no right to judge ourselves. To put it simply, feeling guilty or being overcome with guilt, is not allowed in God's Word. We should not judge either others or we ourselves.

False Guilt Stops Growth

Sometimes our false guilt is so strong it stops our emotional growth. It can actually prevent use from having a relationship with others and with God. Because we are all sinners, the Bible makes clear that level or the degree of sin is irrelevant from God's perspective. We all fall short of the glory of God. However, guilt can sometimes prevent us from seeking God's presence. We're embarrassed by what we have done or ashamed of it, so we wonder how anyone including God can forgive us. We don't even go into God's house (church) because of the sense of, "How could God love me?"

Putting an End to Our False Guilt

False guilt ends when we label it and choose to make it end. We can do that through seeking God by study of the Bible through discussions with others in our situation, owning our behavior, commitment to do better, and prayer. We can learn to unlock ourselves and our thoughts from the judgments of others, or how we believe they may judge us. This takes time practice and prayer, but it can be done. This will put an end to our harsh feelings of paralysis, or "I'm not worthy." This will then free us for dealing with our real guilt before God.

Ending Real Guilt

> If my people who are called by my name humble themselves, and pray and seek my face and turn from their wicked ways, then I will hear from heaven and will forgive their sin and heal their land (2 Chronicles 7:14).

Note the steps in this passage:

- Humble ourselves, and prayerfully seek God.
- Acknowledge our sins, and repent.
- Commit to Jesus as our savior.
- Know that his forgiveness is real.

It is important to notice the similarity of dealing with false paralyzing guilt and dealing with real guilt from God's perspective. The actions prescribed in the Bible are the same! Also, as Jesus followers, if we can accomplish these things, we can know God's peace as peace that passes understanding.

> If we confess our sins, God is faithful and just to forgive us our sins and to cleanse us from all unrighteousness (2 John 1:9).

> There is therefore now no condemnation for those who are in Christ Jesus (Romans 8:1).

Summary

Both false guilt and real guilt require similar actions. God's Word tells us not to judge ourselves but to know that we are imperfect. And that God's grace makes us whole and perfect before him. While we are all guilty (all fall short), the grace of Jesus mak es us perfect to stand before our God. Perhaps this old hymn is the best answer to that.

> Wonderful grace of Jesus, reaching the most defiled.

> By his transforming power, making him Gods' dear child.

> Purchasing Peace and Heaven, for all eternity.

> Oh the wondrous Grace of Jesus, reaches even me.

Lesson 13

Our Example: Jesus's Love and Compassion

This past week, I reflected a person's thoughts back to her on a relationship with her husband. I didn't give advice so much as tell her what she'd just told me: to help her clarify her own thoughts. That discussion might lead to a divorce (I don't know), but it did bring into focus for me a question: what does Jesus's love teach us about our relationships?

When we find ourselves in relationships, maybe friendships at work or in our home or loving relationships with our spouse or children, do we sometimes find that our love for them is tested? Do we get impatient? Do we *lose it* when kids do dumb things or get in trouble at school (which of course, is always the teacher's fault)? Do we sometimes say horrible things particularly if they are saying horrible things to us? What can the Bible teach us about love in all of our relationships? What can Jesus's love teach us?

Jesus's Love

> As the Father has loved me, so have I loved you. Abide in my love. If you keep my commandments, you will abide in my love, just as I have kept my Father's commandments and abide in his love. These things I have spoken to you, that my joy may be in you, and that your joy may be full. This is my commandment, that you love one another as I have loved you (John 15: 9–17).

Is our experience of Jesus's love truly a joy? Doesn't God Word just list a bunch of crap that we are not supposed to enjoy (drinking, sex, and parties)? How does following Jesus make us joyful? Does Jesus and his example of how to live fill you with joy? Perhaps it is time to watch how he responded to various persons he encountered.

> And he said to him, "You shall love the Lord your God with all your heart and with all your soul and with all your mind. This is the great and first commandment. And a second is like it: You shall love your neighbor as yourself (Matthew 22: 37–39).

Okay. So we love our neighbors. What exactly does that mean? Do nice things for them? Perhaps help them out somehow?

> So we have come to know and to believe the love that God has for us. God is love, and whoever abides in love abides in God, and God abides in him (1 John 4:16).

What does it mean to abide in God's love? How can we live in love when this world hurts us so badly? Here's a real example. Broken people are most often broken because they were injured emotionally in some way. I dealt with such a person just this past week. She told me, "I'm not going to church. You can take my daughter if you want, but I ain't going!"

When I asked why, she told me of the death of her mother from cancer when she was seventeen. She remembered praying hard for her mother and how many other times she'd prayed for things. Then she said, "God never did nothin' for me."

So I just looked at her and smiled. Then said, "You see me right here. Right? I mean, I'm here, and my wife and I try to help folks just like you. That's why we're talking."

Then she said, "But that's you. Not God!"

Clearly, I've got some work to do there. We do this because God puts broken people in front of me and my wife. Still, this young woman is still talking, and as she sees help coming, she'll open up about her previous pain when she thought God wasn't listening as her mom died.

> A new commandment I give to you, that you love
> one another: just as I have loved you, you also are to
> love one another (John 13:34).

Now that's a tall order. We should love others like Jesus loved us? Really? Wasn't he the boss's son? Couldn't he do this better than all of us anyway? Does that make a difference? Isn't he still our best example for a loving approach to the world?

What Does Love Mean: How Should We Behave?

> But God shows his love for us in that while we were
> still sinners, Christ died for us (Romans 5:8).

Easy to love those who support us and love us. This says we should love those who disappoint us as much as we've disappointed God. Really? How can we love those who hurt us or disappoint us? What about those who hurt us physically? Can we love them too?

> Father forgive them. For they know not what they
> do (Luke 23:34).

This provided the answer. When Jesus was being tortured to death, he said this prayer for his torturers. Did he seek vengeance on them? Did he get angry and say horrible things back to them? Did he try to *get even*? Did he curse them before God?

No! He prayed for them. This is our model of love. Things like vengeance, anger, hatred, and revenge clearly have no place in Jesus's love, so they should have no place in ours.

> But I tell you, love your enemies and pray for those
> who persecute you, that you may be sons of your
> Father in Heaven (Matthew 5:44–45).

This idea is absolutely unique in all world religions—that we should love all persons including our enemies. In fact, I often argue that this is one of the best reasons to choose Christ over all other religions—I want to support a religion that promotes peace and love, not exclusion or hatred of one's *enemies*. Such hate-filled religions (and there are several) do nothing but instill hatred, violence, and war.

But still, how do we love our enemies? What type of man or woman does that?

Maybe John said it best, "We love, because he first loved us" (1 John 4:19). We learn to love by looking to Jesus and his disciples. We know love because we see it in Jesus.

In another familiar passage, Paul gives us the specifics of love.

> Love is patient, love is kind. It does not envy, it does not boast, it is not proud. It does not dishonor others, it is not self-seeking, it is not easily angered, it keeps no record of wrongs. Love does not delight in evil but rejoices with the truth. It always protects, always trusts, always hopes, always perseveres (I Corinthians 13:4–7).

So this is what love is. No boasting, no envy, pride, or self-seeking. No anger and no memory of past wrongs (my wife will tell you that is where I fail—that memory of past wrongs thing). Love is always trusting, open to hope, and always there. This is the description of perfect love and also the essence of Jesus!

Summary

So Jesus's love means we pray for our enemies. That we forgive everyone and never seek revenge. That we love even those who disappoint us. And that we should show love's attributes to others even when we are wronged somehow. Love should bring joy to our hearts and a peace that passes understanding. If we feel that, we are abiding in Jesus's love. If not, then we probably have some work to do with ourselves.

LESSON 14

Our Response to Jesus: Seeking Righteousness

What I Saw on April 25, 2017!

Why were 125 good men, Christian men, kneeling in prayer on April 25, 2017? What were they seeking? These were some of the best men from many churches in our area during an all-day men's worship event. How could they be any better men? Who are they trying to be?

If you asked them, they would say they were seeking a better relationship with God or seeking righteousness in some sense. They wanted to praise God and seek righteousness in order to worship him! But what exactly does it mean to seek God? To seek righteousness?

As always, the Bible provides the answer. The Bible tells us things to do and things to not do to seek righteousness.

> Do not store up for yourselves treasures on earth, where moths and vermin destroy, and where thieves break in and steal. But store up for yourselves treasures in heaven, where moths and vermin do not destroy, and where thieves do not break in and steal. For where your treasure is, there your heart will be also (Matthew 6:19–21).

First seeking righteousness in God's kingdom means everything we do is done with his kingdom in mind. For example, Jesus said it means using the wealth we've been given to store up treasure in heaven instead of spending it on things that don't matter here.

No one can serve two masters. Either you will hate the one and love the other, or you will be devoted to the one and despise the other. You cannot serve both God and money.

Therefore, I tell you, do not worry about your life, what you will eat or drink; or about your body, what you will wear. Is not life more than food, and the body more than clothes? Look at the birds of the air; they do not sow or reap or store away in barns, and yet your heavenly Father feeds them. Are you not much more valuable than they? Can any one of you by worrying add a single hour to your life?

And why do you worry about clothes? See how the flowers of the field grow. They do not labor or spin. Yet I tell you that not even Solomon in all his splendor was dressed like one of these. If that is how God clothes the grass of the field, which is here today and tomorrow is thrown into the fire, will he not much more clothe you—you of little faith? So do not worry, saying, 'What shall we eat?' or 'What shall we drink?' or 'What shall we wear?' For the pagans run after all these things, and your heavenly Father knows that you need them. But seek first his kingdom and his righteousness, and all these things will be given to you as well (Matthew 6:24–33).

It's easy to say "Don't worry!" but for many of us, that is not easy to do. How many of us have worried about not having good enough clothes to wear to go to church?

So How Else Do We Seek God's Righteousness?

Perhaps, instead of worrying about getting money or getting the best clothes (which Jesus tells us not to worry about), maybe we can seek righteousness by being concerned with things that really matter. "How have we served God today? Or have we sought righteousness today?" Also, don't forget "Who have I helped or done a kind thing for today?"

I will help others: One way to seek righteousness is to acknowledge what God has done for us through Jesus. He paid the debt for our sins. So we seek righteousness by repaying the generosity God has shown us by being generous to those in need. Jesus speaks often of helping those less fortunate.

I will choose God's vision for my own future: Paul said, "Seeking God's Kingdom means to fix our eyes not on what we can see but what we can't see" (2 Corinthians 4:16–18).

That means to have an eternal perspective instead of an earthly one. We shouldn't be so concerned with getting everything this world has to offer. Instead, we should be concerned with what the next life will be like. After all, it's the permanent one. This one is only temporary.

I will give myself to God every single day: Paul also said seeking righteousness means offering our whole being as a living sacrifice to God and refusing to conform to the patterns of this world (Romans 12:1–2). Every single day, we should pray and ask the Lord what he wants us to do with our life instead of going off to do our own thing.

So Back to the First Question

So what were those good men doing on their knees? They were seeking God, and therefore, they were becoming better men! They were feeling the presence of God! These are the best men I know, and if I'm smart, I'll make an all-out effort to be like them!

Now let's do what they did. Right now, wherever you are, if there are two or more of you, do this: get on your knees before Almighty God.

For Our Summary: An Exercise

And so we seek righteousness since worship of God is our primary purpose on this earth. Being a member of the church of Jesus is our best approach to seeking righteousness, and just like those men, we can best worship on our knees. Here's an exercise to make that point.

The group should get on their knees in a small circle. Break larger groups into eight to fifteen persons if necessary, but this exercise may be done with a few as three persons. Everyone should then place their right arm on the shoulder of the person to their right, leaning slightly on them. Then all should put their left arm around the back of the person to their left. Finally, everyone should look up. The leader should then point out the following.

In many ways, this position represents success through collective strength and mutual support. Compare this to Christians in a church seeking God or perhaps to an army fighting a desperate battle. Both groups represent people on a mission!

In war, when men are in the trenches, they are dependent on the person to their left. If that person is wounded or falls, it leaves an opening in the line for the enemy to exploit. Not supporting the person on your left can get one killed. In that sense, everyone in the circle must be embracing, supporting the person to their left—to hold them up or help lift them up even if they begin to fall.

Any soldier will tell you that even if you are stronger, your life depends on those persons around you in a desperate firefight! It is your job to hold them up.

However, everyone is likewise dependent on someone stronger. In this exercise, that is represented by the person on your right. You are leaning on them. If that person falls, you fall because no man stands alone.

Finally, being on one's knees suggests a willingness to look up to one's leadership. Every army has leaders higher up the command chain, and all must follow them if any are to survive the battle. It is the same with Christians. Our leader is Jesus, and we are his church. We must follow him or all is lost. Thus, we depend on each other, we lean on each other, we hold each other up, we are held up by each other, and we all look toward Jesus, our commander, our strength, and our Lord.

While we are all down here, Let's do the obvious. Let us pray…

LESSON 15

My Perceptions and Changing My Life

In a Bug's Eye

One tool to create change in our lives is to change our perception. Here's an example: consider how insects see the world. Most bugs see the world differently than we do. You might remember from your science class in school. Bugs see light differently from the way we do. Remember how a prism separates light into different colors? Bugs see light in the blue/purple end of the spectrum better than red/yellow light. They can also see forms of light that we don't. Might this change how they react to the world?

Like bugs, our experiences determine how we perceive the world, and our perceptions, not reality, determine how we act. With a rather unusual background, it might help us to consider how we perceive the world and how those perceptions might limit us. How does being raised in the projects or a trailer park in a poor neighborhood change who we are? How do we perceive things? How does a background of abuse, neglect, or fear change us? Do we trust others like we would if we had more normal backgrounds? Do we love others—can we love others—in a truly normal way? How do we relate to others on the job or as friends?

Lessons in Perception: A Laughing Jesus?

Back in the 1970s, Playboy magazine caused quite a discussion over a picture. Now this is not what you might be thinking! The picture that caused the stir was not a naked woman but a picture of a laughing

Jesus! It wasn't usual for Playboy to include a Jesus image anyway, but what upset a lot of folks in this instance was that Jesus was laughing!

In fact, in most modern images of Jesus (even in movies), there's almost never a time when Jesus is laughing. Instead, he often looks morbid or displeased with the world and everybody in it. Why no humor? Clearly, the man had charisma since many people followed him daily. Did he never even smile?

In some parables, Jesus can be a bit sarcastic, and he is frequently dry-witted. Isn't that funny? Didn't he laugh a bit? Of course, many stories and teachings are all about rewiring how we look at each other, how we look at the world, and how we define what is really real. Clearly, Jesus understood well the power of perception, and he was all about changing the perceptions of his followers. What else could something like "Pray for your enemies" really mean?

Personally, I like an image of Jesus that laughs once in a while, and I do not think it disrespectful in the least to enjoy a laughing Jesus. In fact, I want all my friends—everyone I like—to be happy! I love the laughing Jesus!

St. Paul's Sense of Perception

Here's a Bible lesson on perception, and how changing perception will change behavior.

> When I was a child, I spoke as a child. I reasoned like a child: When I became a man, I gave up childish ways. For now we see in a mirror dimly, but then face to face. Now I know in part, then I shall understand fully (1 Corinthians 13:11–12).

What is Paul saying here? What does he mean, see in a mirror dimly? Is he suggesting that our belief in Jesus forces us to change our perception? What change do you think he was talking about here?

Perceptions and Jesus's Actions

So what else did Jesus say about perceptions? Did Jesus's actions really challenge conventional perceptions on how others in his world saw the world?

Again, Jesus spoke to them saying, "I am the light
of the world; he who follows me will not walk in
darkness but will have the light of life" (John 8:1–3).

Now we must remember that Jesus was a traveling Rabbi with
a group of followers, and as a Rabbi, he knew Jewish law intimately.
Still, unlike other Rabbi, he did not state that following the Law of
Moses would lead to salvation. He stated that he himself was the light
of the world! Here he is saying that following him will change how his
followers see the world and how they interact with the world—not in
darkness but in light!

He provided many other examples on changes in perception as a
basis for changing one's life including suggestions for how his followers
should perceive the scribes and religious authorities of the day, how
they were the *salt of the earth*, how they should handle the issue of
paying Roman taxes, how harshly they should judge a woman who
committed adultery, and many others. For Jesus, changing perception
was the catalyst for changing actions.

Psychology and Perception

Many books have been written that are dedicated to the
psychology of perception, and once again, those basic conclusions in
psychology and science agree with these Bible passages! God's Word is
right on the money in predicting what psychology and science would
one day teach us about perception. It is a fact that humans base our
behaviors on our perception of the world around us and not the reality.
It is a fact that changing our perceptions can and will result in changes
in our behavior. It is also a fact that many of our perceptions may
be faulty or even erroneous. Thus, many of our actions are based on
bad data from our incorrect perceptions. Remember the bug example
above! Think of a bug flying toward what it perceives to be a beautiful
blue light *only to get zapped!* Like that bug, if we perceive something
wrong, our actions in response to it are likely to be wrong and may
even get us killed!

Here's a practical example straight from the school of Rogue
Warriors! I was once talking with a recovering addict—a meth addict
who had been clean for eighteen months because of her involvement

with accountability court (or drug court). She had been placed in accountability court rather than doing time for a drug offense. She was worried about her future and was telling me how many people failed at drug court. She talked about how often other participants finished the 18-month drug court requirements (living with a curfew, frequent drug testing, and micro management of one's life such as where one lives and where one works), graduated from the court supervision, and then returned to their old way of life. They went back to the same set of friends (most of whom were still using) and the same *party-on* social situations. Of course, that led to them using again and being arrested again. Then they were either placed in prison or returned to drug court for another *stint*! Her fear was that she would not *make it* either.

When I asked her why she thought that happened, her answer was simple: "They don't believe that drug court is there to help them. They believe drug court is only there to harass them."

Her answer here is telling. Folks that perceive drug court requirements as merely legal harassment will frequently fail at using drug court to help them get clean and stay clean. In contrast, those who perceive that all the hassle of the drug court requirements is intended to help them beat an addiction frequently succeed! The right perception of drug court will help them build a new life—a changed life. In other words, one's perception of drug court requirements can determine if it works! Perception is everything!

Practical Applications

As an interesting exercise, the next time you face a problem, perhaps a *dark hole* of doubt or depression, a lack of belief in yourself, or a temptation to drink or do drugs, you might consider how you are perceiving that situation or that feeling. Ask how someone with a solid Christian upbringing might perceive it. Do your actions change when you take on a Christian perception? Do you handle tough times differently?

The old phrase "What would Jesus do?" provides another, in fact, a much better platform for perception of challenges in our lives. How would Jesus define our addiction, our temptation, our depression, or our past history of abuse? How would he perceive us? How would he perceive the situation or temptations we are facing?

Rather than be judgmentally cruel or looking at us with untrusting glances as others might do, wouldn't Jesus take our hand and express his love for us? I mean, he even forgave those who tortured him on that cross, right? Wouldn't he forgive us? Hasn't he already done so? Can we use his perception of us to get a new perspective on our temptations and on our past? Can his and our perception help us redefine our future? Wouldn't he hug us and then tell us he loved us?

Of course, we could always just ask him. As I said before, he's sitting right there beside you, right now!

Summary

Loving Jesus and becoming a Jesus follower demands a change in perception. All of these examples suggest a need to change how we perceive the world, and the reality is that when we change our perceptions of the things in the world that hurt us or do damage to us, we will change ourselves and our behaviors. These examples show that love of Jesus demands a higher, a more pure perception, and a different perception of the world and of our place in the world. He demands that we intentionally choose how we perceive our world and that we perceive it in a fashion consistent with God's will. We must then act on the perceptions that he exemplifies. He is showing us the way.

In short, to change our life, we must change our perception and see the world as Jesus does. He is our light!

LESSON 16

Rebuilding My Life without Stress

God's two main promises to his people:

- life everlasting in the presence of God, and
- a mental peace that passes understanding.

W e've discussed these before. When we become followers of Jesus, we are promised these two things along with other benefits of following Jesus. The Bible reaffirms these promises many times, and while a life everlasting in heaven is a wonderful future, many broken people are much more hopeful for mental peace today. So let's begin by asking ourselves, do I have mental peace now? If not, we might want to consider the reason.

Stress Is the Enemy of Peace

The opposite of inner peace is stress, and psychologists have long noted that excess stress is very destructive. Some have called it the *silent killer* since it accompanies almost all fatal or serious diseases. Stress can bring back pain, headaches, and all other types of muscular pain. Almost all cancer patients feel some level of stress, for example, as do patients with other terminal diseases. Of course, many addicts as well as anyone either in or recently out of abusive situations feel stress.

Another surprising thing about stress is that it can be caused by both negative events and positive events. Stress can result from the celebration of a move into a new place or starting college or celebrating one year sober. All are stressful. In fact, too much success in moving forward in life can sometimes stress someone so much that they turn back to their destructive addictions and bad habits.

Finally, we all face major stressors about once a decade after we are twenty-five and much more frequently prior to that. Buying a new house, a divorce, the death of a child or parent, getting a promotion or being fired from a job, and financial stress—all can disrupt lives—and all are dangerous times. For addicts, meeting a goal in one's move toward sobriety—completing accountability court or finishing a program at a halfway house can cause stress. Many of these may involve moving to a new location, and that change alone can cause stress. These are times to be very careful.

In this sense, attaining the inner peace that a firm belief in God provides is even more critical for broken people than for almost anyone else in Jesus's church. Almost all broken people need to experience God's inner peace—the freedom from stress and the ability to deal with stress.

The Mental Peace that Passes Understanding or Inner Peace

Still, doesn't life defeat us all at times? Doesn't life crush us all? Rent or child care can't be paid—you have no money for groceries. Ex-husband or wife nagging you or maybe texting you just to criticize. Your car breaks down, and you can't get to work. Sounds familiar? Does this stress you out?

Have you ever had something so negative happen that you felt at the end of your rope? A horrible decision in court against you? A horrible embarrassment resulting from a family member's bad decisions? Ever known the death of a child? Death of a parent or sibling? A divorce? Breakup with a girl or boyfriend?

Major stressors such as these happen every two to five years for teens and young adults. There are simply more changes in life during your late teens and early twenties. After that, according to psychologists, adults have one of these major stressors every decade or so. Personally, I've had a higher frequency than that. For this reason, everyone needs that inner peace promised by God particularly in difficult times of life. Ask yourself, could I use that peace right now?

So here's a more fundamental question. Can we even find inner peace even though we are broken? When we crash or freeze up in life, will a solid belief in God's promise of peace help? Can God's Word help us find that peace?

As an experiment, I'd suggest you read Psalms 23. Most of us are familiar with this passage, and many have said that merely reading slowly while you reflect on the words can bring one a measure of inner peace. Can those assurances from God help when you face an impossible situation?

Read Psalm 121. Point out that this is another passage that brings many some measure of peace.

Finding Verses that Bring Peace

In Matthew 6:25–33, what does Jesus tell us of stress in this passage? There are many other statements of God's peace in the Bible, and Christians read any or all of these in difficult times. This is inner peace—a peace that is not changed even when harsh life situations come into our life. Here are other examples of Bible passages that have brought peace to millions of people over the centuries; Romans 8:11 or Romans 8:37–39.

Of course, it's one thing to say that reading the Bible can make some of the stress in our lives go away. However, there is solid evidence of this in the Bible itself. Read Philippians 4:4–7. This is Paul's encouragement to other Jesus followers.

However, here's one thing you should know about that encouraging passage. When it was written, Paul himself was in prison and, as some scholars believe, under sentence of death. It makes one ask, how could a man in prison write such letters of encouragement? Clearly, he had inner peace even in the most difficult of circumstances. In these words, Paul sang the praises of Jesus and his church and talked of "Peace that passes understanding…" while he was in prison! What kind of courage is this—to be in prison, under sentence of death, and yet write of encouragement and of deep inner peace?

We may have challenges in life and not know what to do at times. Some broken people have been in jail or prison. But prisons today cannot be compared with the cruelty of being under sentence of death in a Roman prison of 2,000 years ago! No matter what your circumstances, Paul probably had it worse at that moment, yet he experienced inner peace. Kind of makes you want to say, what's his secret?

Again, how does someone in that situation write encouragement to others? Could you do that? Do you have that kind of inner peace? These passages by Paul are proof of a deep well of peace, a foundation of peace which Paul found in following Jesus. This is an internal peace that passes understanding. If becoming a Jesus follower can empower you to feel that, isn't Jesus worth a shot? After all, millions of addicts, abuse victims, stoners, and other broken people have found this peace. Were they all simply liars? Is this for real? I'm telling you that this inner peace can be yours too. Like I said, Jesus is sitting right there beside you (maybe now would be a good time for another chat).

Now you tell me. Which of these promises is more important: life everlasting or inner peace right now? Which is most important to you? Which means the most to me or to you, we broken people, right now?

Finding Inner Peace: A Plan

So maybe you don't feel it. Maybe those readings are just words for you right now. You've been promised help before and found that it boiled down to simple *BS*. You might as well ask, where is this peace of God for me? Am I honest enough to admit that I don't really feel that inner peace right now? Where do I get that peace? Where do I see this peace of God? Where do I see God's love? What's the evidence? Where have I felt God's love? Where do I see in others God's love?

Paul's secret, if you want to call it that, was simple. Paul's inner peace came from *Jesus's role model* on how to live. When we first hear of Paul in the Bible (early book of Acts), Paul was persecuting Christians. At that point, Paul was an angry, vicious man who thought he was defending the faith of Judaism, but he was really lost in hatred and anger. Then he met Jesus and committed all he was to following Jesus. He then found the secret.

Jesus showed Paul and all of us that inner peace comes from serving others in whatever form you can wherever you are. Giving of your money, your time, your attention, your skills, and all the other things that make you *you*! Giving these things to God, which usually means giving them to others whom God places before you, will bring you deep satisfaction, a well of inner peace, and that peace will help make you secure even when tough times come in life—when the stressors show up! In fact, once you achieve that peace, you will then feel happy possibly for the first time in a while!

The Plan

So here's the question: do I act like Jesus? Where have I shown God's love or God's peace to others? Where do I show his compassion? What caring do I show others right now in life? Do I invest my time and money making lives of others better? Do I give of myself? Perhaps we need a plan to experience Jesus's peace.

Pray. The first step is to pray daily. In fact, pray many times a day. Here's a good one to begin with! "God, help me to cope and let me turn my troubles over to you, but while I'm still troubled, put someone before me that I can help."

Read: Next read the Bible passages above repeatedly. Set a time daily to read at least one of them. You might also read other faith-based literature that brings you peace.

Seek God. Next seek God actively. Be in his house. Find ways to serve him by taking others with you. I know one man from a halfway house that once told me he never came to church without asking at least one other man from the house to come along (and this guy came every Sunday). That's helping others find God. When you feel down, get up and do something nice for someone else for no reason at all!

Be around other seekers. Isolation is the best ally of stress. Being alone is painful and can kill you. How many broken people die by suicide each year because they didn't reach out to others? Thus, to seek God, simply be around others who are facing similar struggles while they and you seek Jesus's love and compassion. Encourage others, and you will be blessed with inner peace.

Call On Others: Reaching out is more than important—it is critical. Use those in this group and in your house or your church as a resource and call them! Do not allow yourself to face the darkness of your past alone. Jesus is always there with you. Paul felt that in his prison cell and you can too.

Summary

Most broken people agree that finding inner peace is something they desire, probably because we carry around so much stress. The good news is that being a Jesus follower does bring one peace, and if you are not sensing that, the steps above will help you develop that peace much like Paul did. Jesus is here with us, and sensing his presence daily and doing his work in the steps above will move you toward a deep well of inner peace: the peace that passes understanding.

LESSON 17

Learning Forgiveness

Most of us have had others work against us, hurt us, or be cruel to us, and at some point, those persons may ask for forgiveness. For those who experienced abuse as a part of their background, great harm may have been done to us by someone who then asks for forgiveness. This lesson explores what forgiveness is, what it means in our lives, and how it might help us free ourselves from our broken past. Should we forgive? When? How often? Let's look to Jesus for those answers.

The Biblical Demand for Forgiveness

> Bear with each other and forgive one another. If any of you has a grievance against someone. Forgive as the Lord forgave you (Colossians 13:3).
>
> For if you forgive other people when they sin against you, your heavenly father will also forgive you. But if you do not forgive others their sins, your father will not forgive your sins (Matthew 6:14–15).

What do we learn from these verses? How are these verses different? While both share the expectation of Christian forgiveness, doesn't the last verse hold a danger for mankind? What is that danger? How might that danger manifest itself?

Forgiveness, Nonforgiveness, and Brokenness

What happens if we forgive others according to the Bible verses above? What happens if we do not forgive? Is it possible that a refusal to forgive others does us damage? Is that possibly what these Bible verses are getting at?

Psychologists often argue that not forgiving someone captures us within the previous injury. Nonforgiveness gives power to the injury and to those who offend against us. Sometimes long after those persons are gone from our lives. In that sense, an unwillingness to forgive is actually injurious to us. In fact, it is not an exaggeration to say that nonforgiveness captures us within our brokenness. Nonforgiveness extends and strengthens that ever-present darkness in our lives. Thus, once again, the Bible is saying the same thing modern psychology is saying—that forgiveness is healthy for us and allows us to move past our brokenness and toward the inner peace we all desire.

You might want to ask yourself at this point, is that true in my experience? Does not forgiving someone actually harm me? Am I captured by nonforgiveness? Am I actually hurting myself through nonforgiveness?

Here's a recent movie example that addressed this theme. "The Shack" is a story about a man who abandoned his rather casual belief in God when his young daughter was abducted. She was raped and killed, and they did not even find her body. The man, enraged at the type of *animal* that would do such a thing, is haunted daily, and in his pain, he begins to destroy his relationship with his other kids and his wife.

Then one day, he receives an invitation apparently from God Almighty to visit the shack in the woods in which his daughter was held prior to her death. Not knowing what to expect he goes, and God actually shows up at the shack, appearing in three persons, Father/Mother, Son, and Holy Ghost. Jesus helps the man understand forgiveness, and he then asked a man to forgive not only his own abusive father but also the horrible man who stole, raped, and killed his daughter.

Is such forgiveness possible? What does that type of forgiveness even mean to those of us who have been repeatedly abused or neglected? What does that type of forgiveness mean for those who injured us? Can this really be God's will that we forgive even as Jesus forgave us? Can any of us possibly do that?

What Do We Forgive?

Are we to forgive all things even those most horrible of things that caused our brokenness? Is there really no offense that is unforgivable? How much forgiveness is demanded of us? What does Jesus expect?

> Then Peter came up and said to him, 'Lord, how often will my brother sin against me, and I forgive him? As many as seven times?' Jesus said to him, 'I do not say to you seven times, but seventy times seven' (Matthew 8: 21–22).

Of course, Jesus did not mean this as the actual number 490. He didn't mean we must forgive 490 times but cling to injury number 491! No, here, Jesus meant we are to forgive all things no matter how many times the evil occurred. Again, do you think that is even possible for mere mortals like us? Is it possible for Rogue Warriors who have seen hell from the inside? Who have been injured repeatedly? Suppose we do try and forgive all. Doesn't that mean the perpetrator of evil gets off completely?

But Do We Do Nothing?

> Pay attention to yourselves! If your brother sins, rebuke him, and if he repents, forgive him, and if he sins against you seven times in the day, and turns to you seven times, saying, 'I repent,' you must forgive him (Luke 17: 3–4).

What element does this verse add to the concept of forgiveness? What does this teach us about how to forgive? Here, it says, we have the right to *rebuke* those who injure us. This begs the question, how should we *rebuke* those who commit wrongs against us? Of course, our example is Jesus. He had the inner peace we all seek, so doing what he did should move us in that direction.

Jesus frequently rebuked his disciples but always with loving kindness. He was always honest but only rarely harsh. In fact, the only example of Jesus's anger in the Bible was when he turned over the tables of the money changers in the temple.

So can we do the same? Can we rebuke with loving kindness and compassion? Does the Bible give us lessons on how we might do that? Let's consider Jesus's prayer from the cross for forgiveness of the soldiers who tortured and killed him.

> Father forgive them. For they know not what they
> do (Luke 23:34).

This is the ultimate forgiveness—a prayer that Almighty God forgive the men who are torturing one to death. Is that type of forgiveness even possible for us as Christians? That discipline, the strength of the mind that can master such forgiveness, *that* is a mind filled with inner peace. This is the level of forgiveness God wants from us since he desired that all of us live and abide within his peace.

Summary

God's demand for us to forgive repeatedly all things seems very harsh, if not outright impossible. However, as believers, we know that God is not some tyrant in the sky making meaningless demands of his minions. Rather, God loves us all and wants the very best for us. In fact, he often shows his love through us and our actions. Therefore, when he demands forgiveness from us, he does so because of what forgiveness means for us.

The Bible clearly states that we have a right to rebuke those who are cruel to us, but we are then called on to forgive. And through forgiveness, we glean so much more. With forgiveness, we are empowered to escape the abuse, to leave behind the hatred, the anger, and the injury. At that point, we can access these experiences and use them to the benefit of others in God's plan. We might even glean wisdom from those injuries, and certainly, as we discipline ourselves throughout life to practice this type of loving forgiveness, we eventually attain inner peace. Thus, forgiveness does, through the example of Jesus, empower us!

LESSON 18

Celebrating My Success

Making Myself Stronger, Making Myself Happy!

Celebration is a critical part of Christian life. In traditional families, all birthdays, anniversaries, and holidays are celebrated. Singing, eating, and telling family stories are the rule, and those celebrations enrich the experience of the family. Thus, these celebrations teach many Christians who they are. However, in nontraditional families, celebration of birthdays, holidays, or anyone's successes is not always a priority. Sometimes birthdays or Christmas or Easter are not celebrated at all. They may not even be mentioned in broken families.

I've had some Rogue Warriors share that they remembered a Christmas as a child with no celebration of Jesus's birth, no presents and no family get-together. During the raging addiction of one parent or both, such celebrations are often overlooked or forgotten altogether. Thus, many people don't understand the critical nature of these celebrations as life- affirming events. I think for this reason, broken people do not seem to celebrate anything; they may provide a birthday party for their own child, but they often allow their own birthday to slip by without mentioning it to anyone.

We might consider the example of the 12-step programs. Every 12-step program celebrates many accomplishments. For example, one gets a token for one day, one week, one month, or one year sober. These programs teach one to celebrate loudly and publicly as they should because any success in life that moves us forward—moves us in a positive direction within God's will—is a success for God's kingdom.

Further, celebrating our successes makes us happier and serves to identify future goals. In the same fashion that we move away from bad habits and destructive behaviors, we must move toward God's will for us, and we must learn to celebrate every step of the way including all the small steps. Thus, celebrating is God's will and is a very appropriate thing to do. Celebrations are part of overall happiness, but unfortunately, celebration is alien to many broken people.

Celebrating Life-Giving Dates

The Bible speaks of many celebrations, and from these, we see the types of things we should celebrate.

> Also you shall observe the Feast of the Harvest of the first fruits of your labors from what you sow in the field; also the Feast of the Ingathering at the end of the year when you gather in the fruit of your labors from the field (Exodus 23:16).

> You shall celebrate the Feast of Weeks, that is, the first fruits of the wheat harvest, and the Feast of Ingathering at the turn of the year (Exodus 34:22).

Clearly, God's Word demands celebration from his people. For an ancient agrarian people such as the Israelites, harvests were not mere opportunities to celebrate. Rather, a good harvest was a life-changing event. Should such a thing warrant God's instruction to celebrate? The answer is a resounding *yes*!

In fact, virtually all ancient peoples in the Bronze Age and the Iron Age celebrated these times of year. These celebrations arose when humans moved from hunter/gatherer societies to early agrarian societies. Good harvests meant that the people would have food throughout the following winter, so those good harvests held the promise of survival! This certainly warranted celebrations!

Celebrating God in Our Worship

But God's Word demands other celebrations also. Here are some more examples.

> Now it was told King David, saying, 'The Lord has blessed the house of Obed-edom and all that belongs to him, on account of the ark of God.' David went and brought up the ark of God from the house of Obed-edom into the city of David with gladness. And so it was, that when the bearers of the ark of the Lord had gone six paces, he sacrificed an ox and a fatling. And David was dancing before the Lord with all his might, and David was wearing a linen ephod. So David and all the house of Israel were bringing up the ark of the Lord with shouting and the sound of the trumpet (2 Samuel 6:12–15).

The Ark of the Covenant was a chest that held the original stone tablets on which the Ten Commandments were written. Thus, it was the most holy symbol of God the Israelites had. Moving it to the area which would become God's holy City of Jerusalem for the first time warranted celebration.

> Then all the elders of Israel came, and the priests took up the ark. They brought up the ark of the LORD and the tent of meeting and all the holy utensils, which were in the tent, and the priests and the Levites brought them up. And King Solomon and all the congregation of Israel, who were assembled to him, were with him before the ark, sacrificing so many sheep and oxen they could not be counted or numbered (1 Kings 8:3–6).

This is another celebration of moving the Ark. Here, Solomon, David's son and the next ruler of Israel, moved the Ark to Mount Moriah, the mount that would be the home of God's temple in Jerusalem. Again, a celebration is demanded including the sacrificing of sheep and oxen.

> Solomon offered for the sacrifice of peace offerings, which he offered to the Lord, 22,000 oxen and 120,000 sheep. So the king and all the sons of Israel dedicated the house of the Lord (1 Kings 8:63).

In this passage, the new Temple of God in Jerusalem has been completed, and this celebration is the dedication of the temple to God. This demands yet another celebration.

Of course, we, broken people, sometimes fixate on weird things, so I'm personally wondering, you know, just out of curiosity, how long would it take to kill 120,000 sheep and 22,000 oxen? But let's get back to the point. As these passages show, these are several celebrations of God's presence among his people. Clearly, God wants us to celebrate holy things, and through such celebrations, we define our lives and build a closer relationship with God.

Celebrating Jesus's Love: The New Testament Covenant

However, Jesus's life represents a new relationship with God. Paul describes this as the New Covenant. Thus, for Christians, this means we celebrate several holidays associated with Jesus's life such as Christmas and Easter. However, there are other times to celebrate our relationship with God!

> But the father said to his slaves, 'Quickly bring out the best robe and put it on him, and put a ring on his hand and sandals on his feet; and bring the fattened calf, kill it, and let us eat and celebrate; for this son of mine was dead and has come to life again; he was lost and has been found.' And they began to celebrate (Luke 15: 22–24).

This is one of the most famous celebrations in the Bible—when the troubled son (a great example of a broken person, by the way) humbly returned home. In this case, Jesus is teaching about a celebration of family values and using that to discuss not the individual family but also the church family. We might consider why Jesus told that story of celebration. What was Jesus's sense of why they were celebrating? Here's another, perhaps, even more important example: the Lord's Supper.

> For as often as you eat this bread and drink the cup, you proclaim the Lord's death until He comes (1 Corinthians 11:26).

The celebration of the Lord's Supper is the most important celebration among Christians. What is celebrated with the bread and cup? This is the celebration of Jesus as victorious over our sin and even his victory over death. It is interesting to note here that while the Bible does not tell us to celebrate Christmas, it does, in this passage, specifically tell us to celebrate the resurrection of Jesus what we now call Easter Sunday. What might that mean? Is Easter a more important celebration than Christmas? For Christians, it certainly is!

Summary

Clearly, God tells us to celebrate important dates in our lives, to celebrate events that bring us closer to God, and to celebrate the new covenant of Jesus's love and the forgiveness of our sins. It is not an overstatement to say that the Bible is filled with celebrations and instructions to celebrate even the smallest things that affirm life and God's love for us. Thus, one task we must learn to do is celebrate the things and events in our life that move us forward and that are consistent with God's will for us. In this fashion, do we honor God. *In short, celebrations please God, make us happier, and mark our direction for ourselves and others. We must learn to celebrate our successes!*

LESSON 19

Grace vs. Works: Accepting God's Gift

What does it mean to be a Christian? What does it mean for a Rogue Warrior to be a Christian? For many of us, our life up to this point has been anything but uplifting! Maybe that makes the question even more important for us, so here's a few things to consider.

What should a Christian life look like? Can we tell who is a Christian by looking at him or her? Can we tell Christians by what they do by their work for God? Should we serve in the local soup kitchen? Build houses for Habitat? Give money to the poor at Christmas? What do these good works reveal about us as Christians? Are we better Christians if we do these things? Are we more *saved* or more committed to God than others?

One running theme in the Bible is the apparent debate on what brings us God's salvation. Are we saved by God's good will, by his grace alone, or does how we act bring us into God's good will? Does what we do after we receive his grace help us express our belief in him?

In the book of James, the emphasis is on works done by the follower of Jesus. However, Paul's writings stress that men are saved by the grace of God alone—that no one can *work* their way into heavenly glory no matter how hard they work or how wonderful a person they might be. So here is the theological question. Is our salvation by faith in the grace of Jesus alone, or must that faith be supplemented by good works? Some might believe that eternal life is based at least in part on doing a certain list of good deeds or serving the organization with time or money. This debate has raged for centuries, and getting into this discussion can help us grow as a Christian, a Jesus follower.

Paul's View: By Grace Alone

Paul was a superstar in the early church! He was one of the best at spreading the Word of Jesus. While there is debate on who wrote what, some believe that Paul is the author of over one third of the New Testament books (eleven of the twenty-seven books in the New Testament). Thus, he was one of the most important men in the Bible and greatly influenced early Christian belief.

Now the major theme of Paul's letters is that salvation is a totally free gift given to us by God's grace alone. Thus, our salvation, our inner peace, and our life everlasting, is a gift and is not earned by our own good works or by following Christian rituals or by obeying laws. Eternal life is given to us by God's grace, and Paul, who was absolutely overwhelmed by that grace, believed that we should show our acceptance of that gift by our faith in Jesus. Paul uses Abraham's life to consider this issue of good works.

> Was it because of his good deeds that God accepted him…from God's point of view Abraham had no basis at all for pride (Romans 4:2).

In Paul's view, God had declared Abram (Abraham) righteous because of his faith, not because of any good deeds Abraham had done. Thus, Paul says that God is gracious in his grace to his followers.

> God justifies 'him who believes in Jesus… By what law? of works? Nay: but by the law of faith (Romans 3: 26–28).

So according to Paul, do we have to do good works in order to be saved, or are we just *saved*? Do we have to tithe? Should we give to the poor or help others? If we don't, aren't we still saved by God's grace?

James' View: A Christian Life Demonstrates Good Work for God

Now over the centuries, many theologians have contrasted Paul's view with that of James. As mentioned earlier, James was, by most accounts, the half brother of Jesus. He was known to be the leader of the church in Jerusalem after the resurrection of Jesus. This gives James a high level of apostolic authority. In short, what he says goes! Thus, it is interesting that in some ways, his one letter in the Bible seems to contradict Pauls' assertion that we are saved by grace alone.

> Ye see then how that by works a man is justified, and not by faith only (James 2:24).

> Though a man say he hath faith, and have not works, can faith save him? (James 2:14),

> Even so faith, if it hath not works, is dead (James 2: 17).

> But wilt thou know, O vain man, that faith without works is dead (James 2:20).

Seems pretty clear here, doesn't it? For James, good works were the mark of the Christian, and without them, faith was *dead*!

So What Does This Mean for Us?

So are these views completely contradictory? What about a sorry, sinful man, who, on his deathbed, says, "Jesus, I have been a horrid sinner, but I believe in you. Please save me." Is that man saved? Does he go to heaven like committed Christians? In short, if we are saved by grace, can't we do anything we want and still be saved for eternal life?

Many religious leaders have suggested that Paul and James were not contradicting each other, so much as emphasizing different aspects of Christian belief. Paul, in his writing, was stressing the gift of our eternal life and Jesus's sacrifice to make our relationship with God right. When God sews his Spirit and his Word into our hearts, we can expect divine fruit to be produced i.e. good works. Just as God's grace pours abundantly upon our lives, our works will then overflow as blessings into the lives of others.

In contrast, James was stressing the practical aspects of faith and how strong faith will lead to sincere work in and for God's kingdom. James was talking about the distinction between false faith (a deathbed conversion) and a working life of faith—a true faith in God's grace and love for us. That saving faith will produce a changed life. A person who is saved is trusting Christ alone for their salvation, not their works.

However, once saved by grace alone, a true <u>Christian</u> will want to practice good works such as feeding the poor and helping others.

The Christian does this not to *earn* salvation which they already have but because they are saved. Being saved means understanding and sharing Jesus's compassion and his love for others, and that compassion leads to good works.

So as broken people, we might want to ask, what have I done for anyone else lately? How does my life reflect the fact that I'm a Jesus follower although perhaps a recent Jesus follower? What can I do right now, even in my sorry state of brokenness, for Jesus's kingdom? For Jesus's other followers, how can I help?

Summary

When God plants his Spirit and his Word into our hearts, we can expect divine fruit to be produced i.e. good works. No matter what state we find ourselves in—in jail or still captured by an addiction, we are Jesus's followers, and as such, we will seek to do his will for others. Just as God's grace pours abundantly upon our lives, our works will then overflow as blessings into the lives of others.

LESSON 20

Why Do Bad Things Happen?

Why do bad things happen in this world? Another way to ask this is why does God let bad things happen? I mean, he's in control, right? So why do bad things happen? Some theologians call this the *problem of evil*. If God made everything and controls everything, why did he create evil things (Another way to say why do bad things happen!)?

I had a recent chat with a man recovering from a meth addiction, whose 4-month-old son died with SIDS. He's mad at God and can't bring himself to come to church. He's mad because of a horrible experience—the death of his son, and he's asking with some anger why does this kind of thing happen? Why do children die of cancer at two or three years old? Aren't they innocent? What kind of God does that? What would you say to that? How would you convince someone of the value of coming to church or worshiping God with other Christians who had had that experience?

For those of us with broken lives, we may find ourselves saying that even more than others. When persons were abused at an early age or became addicts quite early, they often challenge God with the question, "Why me, God?" Have any of you ever asked that question?

There are as many answers to this question as there are people who care to engage in theological dialogue. Most Christians refer to a larger plan of God's that we do not now understand. Perhaps such tragedy has meaning to someone else in some fashion that we are unaware of. Another idea is that yes, God allows *bad* things to happen, but God does not cause them to happen. What does that really mean?

While answers are hard to come by on this question, one thing we can be certain of is that bad things, inexplicable things, do happen. In fact, Jesus himself said they *are* coming. Unlike Buddhists who often write off pain and suffering as just being illusions, Jesus was honest. He told us the truth. He didn't say you might experience bad things in life. He said it *is* going to happen.

You will have suffering in this world (John 16:33).

We Have Freedom!

One valid answer to these questions is that we have freedom. We have to understand that God wants his people to have freedom, radical freedom, in the sense that we can even choose to not believe in God. In that sense, we are free people, not puppets on a string. As free individuals, we have to accept that sometimes bad things result from our own bad choices (not always but sometimes). In that sense, God does not cause *bad* things to happen. In fact, our choices may play a role, and in those cases, it helps to know that Jesus still loves us and grieves with us in our pain when *bad things* happen.

Therefore, we might best respond by saying that God does not will *bad* things to happen in life. Rather, *bad* things happen in the freedom that comes to us with the gift of life. When *bad* things happen to any of God's children, God is grieved and suffers with us, experienced most vividly in the hurt and suffering of Jesus Christ for all humanity.

Of course, as Jesus's death and resurrection show, any *bad* thing which happens is never the last word. Jesus's death was not his end! Rather, a resurrection for him and for us into eternal life is the final word for Jesus followers. In another way of saying it, God is the deepest and last word, and that word is love and eternal life with God.

We Are Not God!

Another answer to this question is that God's plan is much larger than our individual lives. None of us has God's understanding of the miracle of this universe, and we don't have God's mind or see with God's perspective. The Bible makes that clear when Paul says:

Now we see things imperfectly, like puzzling reflections in a mirror, but then we will see everything with perfect clarity. All that I know now is partial and incomplete, but then I will know everything completely, just as God now knows me completely (I Corinthians 13:12).

So we should expect to have an incomplete perspective on why things happen, including painful and very personal things. We can't understand everything from our finite perspective. When we ask about specific individual events and want to know why this particular thing happened, we won't get the full answer in this world. Someday we'll see with clarity, but for now, things are foggy as Paul said in the passage above.

Of course, for people in tragedy who are in great pain, this type of theological discussion is completely insufficient. In fact, any intellectual response is going to seem trite and inadequate. Perhaps a better response when someone asks these questions can be found in the Bible.

How Should Christians Help Others in Pain?

People in acute pain don't need a philosophical discussion or God's plan of human freedom within that plan. When people ask these questions about bad things and painful things, what they need to experience is Jesus's love and compassion. They need, at that moment, a sympathetic hearing, a response from one's heart, a response that shows Jesus's gentleness, compassion, and love. Generally, they also need to grieve, and that fact should let other Christians know how to help in those painful times. Persons in great pain desperately need the very real and comforting presence of Jesus Christ in their lives. How, then, do we share the peace of God with someone in great pain or even with someone who might be mad at God? Here is a plan that will usually help.

Listen. First listen to the person in pain. Jesus listened to everyone he dealt with—from the lowest prostitute to the highest ranking priests and rulers. We should listen too. Listening and repeating to someone their own perspective is critical to letting them know they have been heard and taken seriously. Also, repeating the issue and their thoughts back to them helps you understand what is really going on and may help them hear their own emotions and issues in a different way.

Sympathize. Offer sympathy. Cry with them or lend them your shoulder to cry on. Don't jump into immediate discussion of theology, and don't *one-up* them by sharing your pain or a similar experience you've had. That may be appropriate at some point but is probably not appropriate immediately. Also, remember to continue to listen as you sympathize. Often, a grieving person needs to say the same things in a number of different ways. You must allow that, and listen to the nuances of each example.

Pray. Never underestimate the power of prayer. Prayer can inspire, heal, relieve stress, and promote empathy. Prayer also helps Christians clarify our thoughts before God. Prayer is how we are privileged to communicate with God, and often, it is how God speaks to us. Many times, as we pray about an issue or concern, we begin to sense a direction that seems to be more right than others. God often speaks to us when we pray.

Read. Read the Bible together if and when the time is right during someone's grieving. Don't rush into a Bible reading immediately, but when you sense the person has described his or her feelings several times, you might suggest a passage that helps relieve stress (we've discussed these before). Many passages are familiar to many Christians and many nonchristians, and simply reading these can bring comfort. Psalm 23 or 121 come to mind. The beatitudes in Matthew or the Lord's Prayer will sometimes bring peace and comfort to a troubled heart. Paul's words in Romans Chapter 8 or I Corinthians Chapter 13 are lovely, deeply spiritual passages that often help when persons are in pain. Open the Bible, and read one or more of these, and then ask how that made the other person feel.

Discuss. At some point, the grieving person may indicate a desire to have a theological discussion of why does God let bad things happen. However, this should be the last step in this process and not the first, and it may be a matter of days or weeks before a grieving person is ready for this. Sometimes when a grieving person says, "Why did this happen?" They don't want theology—they want sympathy. So going through the other steps first is critical. Only after that will grieving persons be ready to accept the unknowns involved in God's plan and how we cannot see the whole of that plan.

Summary

No satisfactory answer to the problem of evil or the question "Why would God let this happen?" is possible when someone is in great pain. Neither God's master plan nor God's desire to give us freedom is a complete, sufficient explanation in those difficult times. At that point, the person needs to experience Jesus's love and compassion and empathy, and we, as Christians, must show that. Therefore, having a plan on how to respond to bad things is important for all Christians. The steps above, listen, sympathize, pray, read, and discuss, seem to be the best approach. And beyond that, we can count on God to move in the heart of the grieving person when the time is right.

LESSON 21

How Should I Pray?

Many of us find ourselves praying at difficult times or times when we are hurt. "Lord, please help me with this court case" or "God, let me get out of this relationship, and then find a good healthy relationship in my life." This is understandable since that is when we need God the most and usually seek him through prayer. However, understanding that prayer is or can be more than a cry for help can empower us to use prayer when we may not otherwise think of it.

One of my favorite prayers is the Shepard's Prayer. It is probably not what you might expect.

"Oh Lord, don't let me F— up!"

This was said by Alan Shepard, one of the first American astronauts, while he was waiting atop a rocket for the second manned mission into space by an American. To make matters worse, he said that prayer through an open mike!

While language is inappropriate here, broken people don't pay quite as much attention to bad language, and clearly, the sentiment is real. "God, help me manage this impossible situation!" or "God, give me strength to do and say the right things to calm down this explosive situation." How many times in life have you said a version of this prayer?

In looking at Bible guidelines on how to pray, there are several things to consider, but most of the Bible instructions fall into four areas: A Prayerful Attitude, When to Pray, What to Pray for, and God's Response to Prayer. Let's consider each of these.

A Prayerful Attitude

And when you pray, you must not be like the hypocrites. For they love to stand and pray in the synagogues and at the street corners, that they may be seen by others. Truly, I say to you, they have received their reward. But when you pray, go into your room and shut the door and pray to your Father who is in secret. And your Father who sees in secret will reward you. And when you pray, do not heap up empty phrases as the Gentiles do, for they think that they will be heard for their many words. Do not be like them, for your Father knows what you need before you ask him (Matthew 6:5–15).

If we confess our sins, he is faithful and just to forgive us our sins and to cleanse us from all unrighteousness (1 John 1:9).

I thank my God in all my remembrance of you, always in every prayer of mine for you all making my prayer with joy, because of your partnership in the gospel from the first day until now. And I am sure of this, that he who began a good work in you will bring it to completion at the day of Jesus Christ. It is right for me to feel this way about you all, because I hold you in my heart, for you are all partakers with me of grace, both in my imprisonment and in the defense and confirmation of the gospel (Philippians 1:3–11).

Rejoice in hope, be patient in tribulation, be constant in prayer (Romans 12:12).

So what do we see here about a prayerful attitude? Here, we see instructions to not show off by using big, important words! Just talk to Jesus. We also see the mandate to be close to God. Next we see that we should take joy from God's grace and pray with thanksgiving including praying for other believers. Finally note that we must always confess our sins before God.

When Should We Pray?

> Pray without ceasing (1 Thessalonians 5:17).
>
> Praying at all times in the Spirit, with all prayer and supplication. To that end keep alert with all perseverance, making supplication for all the saints (Ephesians 6:18).
>
> I desire then that in every place the men should pray, lifting holy hands without anger or quarreling (1 Timothy 2:8).

This answer on when to pray is simple: pray anytime and anywhere and everywhere! I do this with what I call *shotgun prayers*. I shoot out a whole bunch of quick one-sentence prayers almost every day!

Of course, I've heard other Christians, Christians whose faith I believe inand respect, say things like, "I pray for at least thirty minutes every eveningjust before bed." While I admire that *that* has never been me. I'm more of a shotgun guy. If you don't know, a shotgun doesn't fire a single bullet like a pistol or a rifle. Rather, it tosses out scores or hundreds of pellets seemingly in all directions. That's how I pray— tossing up one-line or two-line prayers many, many times daily. I hear an argument between co-workers, and I'll toss up a prayer, "God, help me manage this and let me know if you want me involved at all!" Then I do what I think best. Sometimes it is to stay out of that business, but other times, it means I try to intervene with the right words or actions.

Other shotgun prayers I've done many times:

> God, that is the most beautiful mountain creek I've ever seen. Thanks for that.
>
> Lord, I've pissed off my wife pretty bad, and I don't know how. Please help.
>
> God, I'm driving over to a tough meeting. Let me say the right things, and let me live with the results whichever way it turns out.
>
> God, I'm mentoring a kid this morning. Help me improve his reading.

God, I'm talking to 200 people today. Let me share something they can use and in a way they enjoy. Thanks.

I'll toss up ten to twenty prayers in any given day, sometimes many more. Probably too many of them are cries for help, but that's me. I did say I was Broken, just like you. Is anybody else a shotgun prayer person?

What Should We Pray for?

> Now Jesus was praying in a certain place, and when he finished, one of his disciples said to him, 'Lord, teach us to pray, as John taught his disciples.' And he said to them, 'When you pray, say:
>
> 'Father, hallowed be your name. Your kingdom come. Give us each day our daily bread, and forgive us our sins, for we ourselves forgive everyone who is indebted to us. And lead us not into temptation (Luke 11:1–5).
>
> Therefore, confess your sins to one another and pray for one another, that you may be healed. The prayer of a righteous person has great power as it is working (James 5:16).
>
> First of all, then, I urge that supplications, prayers, intercessions, and thanksgivings be made for all people, for kings and all who are in high positions, that we may lead a peaceful and quiet life, godly and dignified in every way (1 Timothy 2: 1–2).
>
> Do not be anxious about anything, but in everything by prayer and supplication with thanksgiving let your requests be made known to God (Philippians 4:6).

The Bible is quite clear. As Christians, we are invited to pray for any desire we have and any requests we have. We should also pray to confess our sins and then pray for forgiveness. We must pray for others and pray with thankfulness. Finally we should often pray just to praise God.

God's Response to Us

> Whatever you ask in my name, this I will do, that the Father may be glorified in the Son (John 14:13).

> And this is the confidence that we have toward him, that if we ask anything according to his will he hears us (I John 5:14).

> The Lord is not slow to fulfill his promise as some count slowness, but is patient toward you, not wishing that any should perish, but that all should reach repentance (2 Peter 3:9).

> As you come to him, a living stone rejected by men but in the sight of God chosen and precious, you yourselves like living stones are being built up as a spiritual house, to be a holy priesthood, to offer spiritual sacrifices acceptable to God through Jesus Christ (1 Peter 2:4–6).

God has committed to answer our prayers. However, he doesn't necessarily give us all we ask for. First of all, God's time for answering prayer is not our time. Next God's plan is much larger than what we can see during our lifetime. His will is much larger than our will, and he knows things that we don't. Thus, his answer to our prayer may not be what we expect. What we can be certain of is it is consistent with God's overall plan.

Summary

In summary, the Bible gives us many instructions on how to pray. We are instructed to pray all the time about all matters that we wish to bring before God. We should pray humbly in secret and together as Christians with thankfulness and humility and faith. We should pray for each other, and let prayer strengthen our bonds together. We should pray with faith and stand in a right relationship to God as we pray. Maybe if we do this right and practice a lot, one day, we can count ourselves as abiding in the peace of God.

LESSON 22

The Power of Prayer

Like the lesson above on bad things happening, there are times in life when everything goes wrong. Often at those times, we begin to understand the reality that God is our only option. This happens sometimes when we are down and out, worried about something or simply scared. Broken people know this feeling all too well. For a Jesus follower, that is when many of us pray our most earnest prayers.

It might help to ask, why do we hear so much about the power of prayer in the Bible? What exactly is prayer? Is it reasonable to hope for the things we pray for?

The Power of Prayer

> Therefore, I tell you, whatever you ask in prayer, believe that you have received it, and it will be yours (Mark 11:24).

> Whatever you ask in my name, this I will do, that the Father may be glorified in the Son. If you ask me anything in my name, I will do it (John 14:13–14).

> Do not be anxious about anything, but in everything by prayer and supplication with thanksgiving let your requests be made known to God. And the peace of God, which surpasses all understanding, will guard your hearts and your minds in Christ Jesus (Philippians 4:6–7).

Some of these verses have shown up in this book before, including several from last week's lesson. Still, here we must ask, what do these verses say of the power of prayer? Is there any limit to what God can do according to these Scriptures? Now as one broken man to another, I urge you to ask yourself, do I really believe that? Can I believe that? Can I simply choose to believe something like that?

An Example of the Power of Prayer

On February 9, 1991, an American aircraft was shot down in Kuwait On February 10, 1991, they prayed…

We'll call that Marine Lt. Jamie Johnson (not his real name). He was flying a Marine Harrier when he went down that day. As a four-year marine veteran, he'd previously flown a number of combat missions, and that day, he was over Southern Kuwait. He was destroying Iraqi bunkers and artillery, and his bomb delivery only seconds before it was successful. But as he pulled away, his aircraft was hit by an Iraqi surface-to-air missile. The Harrier rolled sharply left, nose down, giving Jamie only moments to save himself. He grabbed the ejection handle to get out and in seconds was hanging below his canopy, gently floating down directly toward the men he's just bombed.

He was captured almost immediately, surrounded by Iraqi soldiers who took him to a nearby bunker where they held him for a while. Later, he was driven to a nearby city where his interrogators began both a series of beatings interspersed with questions. Jamie remembers that "They knew how to inflict pain and how to keep you conscience to feel all." Mercifully, the beatings only lasted for twenty-four hours or so, and Jamie had a *private-survival technique* that kept him sane (more on that a bit later). For all he knew, he would be killed any second when the beatings stopped. In time, however, he was driven to Baghdad and imprisoned in a ten by twelve cell with a number of other American and British flyers. They existed for days on poor rations, stale bread, and fear. They were prohibited from even talking to each other.

In New Bern, North Carolina, Jamie's wife, Renee, was quickly informed that he had gone down on a combat mission. He'd been listed as missing-in-action. Panic is not nearly descriptive enough to express what she felt. It is a poor word, indeed, to adequately describe her fear, her physical ache, and her near paralysis. On that first night, February 9, she fell completely apart. Her husband was down, maybe dead. Then she had to call his parents and tell them the news along with her children. Jamie, at that moment, was still being beaten, halfway around the world. Meanwhile, Renee couldn't sleep at all that Saturday night or well into the early hours of Sunday morning. Sleepless, alone, and in total desperation with nothing left emotionally, she reached out to God.

Around 4:45 a.m. on that Sunday morning, she called her Sunday school teacher in tears and simply asked him to pray for her family and for Jamie.

That's when my brother's phone rang. My older brother Jack was teaching one of the adult couple's classes at the church Jamie and Renee attended. Our family had always lived near the Cherry Point Naval Air Station in Havelock, North Carolina, and Jack then lived in New Bern. He knew them as occasional members of his class, but he didn't feel their faith was deep, a fact that Jamie later confirmed. The marines in that area come and go regularly, and Jack had not had the opportunity to really get to know Jamie or Renee very well.

Jamie was not a committed Christian when he went down as he himself has often said. However, while he was being beaten and when he felt he had no hope to survive, he did what his wife had done. He called out to God. During his torture, Jamie did manage to remember the first line of an old beloved hymn, "Victory in Jesus, my savior forever." He reported that during his beatings, he'd hum or sing that line to himself but only that first line. He said that kept him sane when he had no hope at all.

"Victory in Jesus, my Savior forever..."

When Jack got the call from Renee, he prayed quickly and then woke his wife and told her that Jamie's plane was down in Iraq. Just a bit later that morning, he decided what he had to do. He called every member of that Sunday school class and told them Jamie was down and to get to church as soon as they possibly could. By 8:30 a.m., they had a prayer circle going at church with several of the regular Sunday school classes suspended for that morning. For the next few hours, people would come and go, joining in the circle and offering a prayer as they felt they could. Some merely sat in the circle and cried which can be a prayer in and of itself. That prayer circle continued until Jack called an end around 11:00 a.m.

Meanwhile, halfway around the world, Jamie was still being beaten. And to continue to sustain himself, he still sang that first line and hummed the rest over and over again, "Victory in Jesus, my Savior forever." As far as they could tell after the fact, the prayer circle was ongoing for a time even while Jamie was being beaten during that first twenty-four hours of captivity.

Imagine that rather strange connection for a moment. There are twenty to forty-five members of the Adult Sunday School classes going around the circle and praying repeatedly one after the other and half a world away between beatings, Jamie would mumble to himself, "Victory in Jesus, my Savior forever." One could argue that prayer circle stretched halfway around the globe with Christians together calling out to the Lord God Almighty.

It was a bit later that week that Jamie's face became famous around the world. You may have seen it yourself. After beating him, the prison guards gave him a script denouncing America and had him read it on camera. That footage hit and the international news channels along with footage of four or five other tortured pilots. All military men are under orders to do whatever the prison guards tell them in those situations including reading scripts on camera. At the very least, if they are televised doing so, it shows their families they are still alive.

Well, as was God's will, that was a quick war, and Jamie was freed later that same month, but that's not the end of this story. Jamie shared his new faith often based in no small measure on that one line of the old hymn. Later, in a church wide celebration in April of that year, the whole congregation sang the hymn!

Of course, Jamie and Renee both grew deeply in their faith in this experience, and hearing Jamie tell the story of the power of prayer is beyond amazing. It will change who you are. I asked him to tell it to me once in a private discussion several years later—just Jack, Jamie, and me. It moved me to tears. It is truly powerful beyond words!

Today Jamie, Renee, and their family have moved far beyond New Bern, but they still visit once in a while. His kids are grown now, and his career in the marines has been a phenomenal success. He still proudly serves our country today as a combat veteran, a senior leader in the United States Marines, and most importantly of all, as a Christian!

As you might imagine, both Jamie and Renee, as well as every other member of that Sunday School class, believe absolutely and completely in the power of prayer. As he himself will testify, a prayer circle and an old hymn saved his sanity that day and, perhaps, his life. In fact, everyone involved in that experience will tell of the power of that prayer circle, perhaps with a subtle nod to the strength, the amazing power of that beautiful, old hymn "Victory in Jesus." That hymn and those prayers helped a man and his wife both endure the unimaginable.

For these people, prayer is a real concrete thing. It is a force of nature. Prayer is asking God to directly intervene and to help us, and when we have no other hope, God's power is often our only option. In fact, if we are honest with ourselves, the reality is that in all circumstances, God is really the only option we have. His will rules the universe, and just knowing that we can ask for anything from God is a palpable thing that can bring hope and a measure of peace to anyone and everyone including you! No matter how broken you might be, whether being tortured in a foreign war or existing in your own self-created hells such as addiction, Jesus is there with you every single second. For a Jesus follower, prayer makes his presence real.

Of course, the Bible says it best.

> Ask, and it will be given to you; seek, and you will find; knock, and it will be opened to you (Matthew 7:7).

Summary

Prayer is a joyous communion between you and God. It is the single, strongest force in the universe, and even broken people like us should pray without ceasing. It is a fact in all of our lives as it was in Jamie's that we are stronger when we humble ourselves and pray. Further, we are stronger and more joyful when our prayers take the form of singing praises to God. So together, we shall Sing! Sing out loud if you know this old hymn!

Sing in praise to God!

Sing for Jamie…

Victory in Jesus

I heard an old, old story, how a savior came from glory How he gave his life on Calvary, to save a wretch like me. I heard about his groaning, and his precious blood atoning Then I repented my sins and won the victory!

Chorus

Oh Victory in Jesus, my savior forever

He sought me and bought me with his redeeming blood. He loved me ere I knew Him, And all my love is due Him He plunged me to Victory beneath the cleansing flood.

The Last Verse

I heard about a mansion He has built for me in glory

And I heard about the streets of gold, beyond the crystal sea. About the angels singing, that the old redemption story,

And some sweet day I'll sing up there, my song of victory!

(Repeat the chorus once again for Jamie)

Lesson 23

Blessings of God: Making God Real in Our Lives

When we get up on Sunday and make the effort to get to church, what does that really mean for our lives? Are we supposed to feel different every single Sunday? What if we don't feel different or if we feel nothing at all? Even after we have chosen to accept Jesus, to believe that Jesus is our Lord and Savior, and that his sacrifice made our relationship right with God once again, what does that mean? Are we really supposed to feel God's presence in our lives each day? What if we don't? If we believe, how is our life different?

God's Blessings for Us

We've discussed two blessings from God several times already in this book: eternal life and inner peace. Still, God promises many other blessings throughout the Bible, and we should consider those also.

According to one source, there are over 7,000 promises of blessings from God found in the Bible! First let's read one of the most famous: The Beatitudes in Matthew 5:1–12. The word beatitude means *blessing*, and he promised us several things in that Scripture. We'll consider each blessing individually and personally.

> Blessed are the poor in spirit, for theirs is the kingdom of heaven.

> Blessed are they who mourn, for they shall be comforted. Blessed are the meek, for they shall inherit the earth.

Blessed are they who hunger and thirst for righteousness, for they shall be satisfied.

Blessed are the merciful, for they shall obtain mercy. Blessed are the pure of heart, for they shall see God.

Blessed are the peacemakers, for they shall be called children of God.

Blessed are they who are persecuted for the sake of righteousness, for theirs is the kingdom of heaven (Matthew 5: 3–10).

This is another Bible passage that brings some sense of inner peace to Christians. Read it again slowly as you might read a poem and see if you sense that peace?

Next ask yourself, do any of these blessings speak to you? Have any of us ever felt poor in spirit? Have we ever hungered for righteousness? Have you ever envied a Christian his or her belief? Ever wondered what life would look like if you shared that belief?

If you are doing this Bible study as a group, I want each of you to share by picking the blessing above that most speaks to you and discussing a time in your life when you may have felt poor in spirit or merciful or in mourning, etc.

Upon acceptance of Jesus, our life should have new meaning for all of us because the Bible states that we are blessed by God. If we do not sense those blessings in our lives, we might need to consider why. In fact, if we do not sense God's blessings or his presence each day, we must re-examine our commitment to God.

More Promised Blessings from God

There are many other passages on God's blessings. Numbers 6:24–26 is another very familiar passage on God's blessings for his followers.

The Lord bless you and keep you; the Lord make his face shine upon you and be gracious to you; the Lord turn his face toward you and give you peace.

This is one of those Bible passages that seem to always bring peace to a troubled soul. Read it again slowly, and see if you feel that peace yourself— that passes understanding.

Then consider each of these questions. What does it mean for the Lord to make his face shine upon you and be gracious to you? What might this blessing entail? How do we feel when we hear that being read out loud? Does merely hearing that bring some small measure of peace to our hearts?

What If We Don't Sense God's Blessings?

Still, we are broken people—all of us. Sometimes we are so hardened by our brokenness that we don't allow ourselves to feel peace even when we could. So what do we do if we are not in tune with God's blessings? What do we do if we do not feel God's peace? The Bible provides several things that we should do to sense God's presence in our lives.

Pray without ceasing (1 Thessalonians 5:17)!

We've discussed prayer before in these lessons. As noted previously, prayer is a two-way communion between you and God. Prayer is not merely giving God your daily wish list. Rather when you pray earnestly, you will sincerely tell God about your concerns and then listen to your heart to hear what God might be saying.

Give alms to the poor (Matthew 6:2).

Alms means support, and in today's world, this usually means giving money. It can mean giving time (e.g. serving in a soup kitchen). When was the last time you gave something to someone else without expecting a payback? Even if you have no money, you are expected to give something. All Jesus followers give to others.

> But when you fast, put oil on your head and wash
> your face, so that it will not be obvious to others
> that you are fasting, but only to your Father, who is
> unseen; and your Father, who sees what is done in
> secret, will reward you (Matthew 6:17-18).

Fasting was the ancient practice of going without food for a period of time. While some Christians fast today, fasting is not really a part of most modern Christian traditions. Baptists, as one example, are more used to fried chicken and *dinner on the grounds*! You may have heard the oft- repeated joke: where two or more Baptist are gathered in his name, a chicken must die!

Clearly, Baptists don't fast a great deal.

Still, what is the real message here? Is it fasting or is it perhaps doing God's work in secret? Of course, it is the emphasis on doing God's work without bragging. Christians don't look for *credit* from others or recognition from other Christians. We just serve because that is what Jesus told us to do. Moreover, that is what Jesus did! Maybe the best way to think of this is similar to an old tennis shoe commercial: just do it!

Don't seek glory or recognition, just do the work. By doing the work of God, we will help others, and more importantly, we will sense God in our lives more each day. In that sense, we will experience his blessings more so each day of our lives.

Summary

God promises us many blessings if we follow him, and if we don't sense these, we must re-examine our own lives. We should pray about our desire to feel God's presence in our lives. We should give of ourselves—money, time, effort, and we should do everything we do for God in private. In these ways, we shall see God and feel him in our lives!

LESSON 24

My Total Commitment to God

Commitment is a buzz word in modern society, so much so that the concept is a running joke on TV—the *commitment* problem that some men have when considering a life-long partner, or *commitment* to a job have become sitcom stories that are quite common. More seriously, for the last several decades, the divorce rate has hovered at fifty percent or so. Do that many people in our society have a problem with commitment?

Strangely enough, addicts don't have this *commitment* problem, at least when it comes to their addiction. For addicts, there are times when their only focus is that next high! The high is so central in life for these folks that it is the only concern, a serious commitment! Certainly, no lack of commitment there—at least when it comes to getting high!

Recovering addicts also know about a more positive concept of total commitment: to get clean and stay that way. Almost all addicts, in order to succeed, must make a total commitment to their sobriety. Many, if not most, know that they will fight that battle daily. Sobriety must be a critical commitment on which your very life depends!

That is not dissimilar to a total commitment to God (in fact, this may be one and the same). One addict once told me that he let the cross of Jesus stand between himself and his addiction. When he wanted the next fix or the next high, he literally visualized it. He imaged a cross between that fix and himself. He then reaffirmed each time, his total commitment to that cross, and what it represented for him, that he was a totally new creation in Jesus Christ.

For many life-long Christians, the commitment problem is a bit different. Most Christians have made a commitment to God. The question then becomes: is theirs a total commitment? The Bible makes clear that only a total commitment is acceptable to God. Have you made that total commitment to Jesus?

For some Christians (and I am one of these), the commitment to and belief in Jesus runs from hot to cold. Ministers often note that many persons who join the church and seem *on fire for God* for a while sometimes seem to burn out in mere weeks or months. Those folks then just seem to fade away from their commitment. So next we should ask, what does the Bible say?

> You shall love the LORD your God with all your heart and with all your soul and with all your might (Deuteronomy 6:5).

Do we see that God demands total commitment here? Is that the commitment we see in most Christians? Is that what we see in ourselves, those of us who are broken?

It can be helpful to ask what types of commitment we see in other religions. How about suicide bombers from Islam? Or the Buddhist Monks who burned themselves alive in protest of American actions during the early years of the war in Vietnam? Was that a total commitment to God according to their beliefs? Do we see such commitment among Christians today?

When our belief wanes, that is often reflected in our church attendance or our work for the church or our work for others. What dangers does this entail for us and for others in our family or our circle of friends?

Our Level of Commitment

> Trust in the LORD with all thine heart; and lean not unto thine own understanding (Proverbs 3:5).

> Jesus said unto him, 'Thou shalt love the Lord thy God with all thy heart, and with all thy soul, and with all thy mind' (Matthew 22:37).

Does this give us indication of what God expects our level of commitment to look like? Is this level of commitment even possible for those of us who are broken? And that begs the next question. Would God set an impossible standard for us to emulate? Is that fair?

How Do We Develop Total Commitment?

If our commitment is expected to be complete, how do we do that? Are there things we can do to develop our commitment? As always, we should look to the Bible.

> Be joyful always; pray continually; give thanks in all circumstances, for this is God's will for you in Christ Jesus (1 Thessalonians 5:16–18).

> Let no corrupting talk come out of your mouths, but only such as is good for building up, as fits the occasion, that it may give grace to those who hear (Ephesians 4:29).

> If anyone says, 'I love God,' and hates his brother, he is a liar; for he who does not love his brother whom he has seen cannot love God whom he has not seen (2 John 4:20).

> Brothers, I do not consider that I have made it my own. But one thing I do: forgetting what lies behind and straining forward to what lies ahead (Philippians 3:13).

There are many instructions here on total commitment. Be joyful, pray continually, give thanks in all circumstances, watch what you say, do not hate anyone, forget past wrongs, and look to the future in Jesus. These things are all part of total commitment.

Now Read 2 Timothy 4: 1–2. What does that say about sharing the Word? Clearly, we should spread the Word of Jesus, his love and compassion, in all seasons. This must likewise be considered a part of total commitment. We should spread the Word even as Jesus and his disciples did.

What May We Expect If We Concentrate on Our Commitment?

> Commit your work to the Lord, and your plans will
> be established (Proverbs 16:3).

> I have fought the good fight, I have finished the
> race, I have kept the faith (Timothy 4:6–8).

Both the Old Testament and the New Testament Scripture above, say the same thing. If we are totally committed, God will reward us! We will be victorious. What a blessing it must be to come to the end of one's days and say with Paul, "I have fought the good fight, I have finished the race, I have kept the faith."

Summary

Total commitment is both demanded and expected of us. While *all fall short*, we are still expected to struggle to show commitment. We are instructed to pray, to present ourselves before God as one who works for God, to watch our speech, to make amends to our fellowman, to forgive and leave behind the past, and to preach God's Word all the time whether our commitment is strong or weak. We are told that as we show commitment to others, we will be rewarded both with our plans on this earth and eternally in heaven, so that we, like Paul, may die knowing we have done God's work on earth and have fought the good fight, have finished the race, and kept the faith.

Then in the days of our death, we will behold our Savior, Jesus Christ, even as he smiles at us after we rise in his glory. Then he smiles and says, "Welcome home, my broken one. I've been waiting especially for you!"

LESSON 25

What Does Easter Really Mean?

In light of these recent lessons—prayer, receiving God's blessings, and total commitment to God, we can now ask the ultimate question: what does it all mean?

Of course, some may not realize that this question is summarized in one word: Easter. As the meme on the internet showed each Easter season, "It's not the bunny! It's the Lamb!"

Now I realize that most Rogue Warriors didn't experience Easter like many Christians. What Mom took the time to get candy or chocolate bunnies or color Easter eggs when that Mom's biggest worry was getting high? Many Rogue Warriors, my broken ones, had that latter experience of Easter if they had an Easter experience at all.

Still, most of us know the story of Jesus's trials, his torture, and death on the cross. We know that the early Jesus followers found his tomb empty on that Sunday morning. But what did that do for us? What does Easter really mean for us? How is a 2,000-year-old death by Roman torture meaningful today?

First a Few Facts

Here is a definition of Easter. Easter is the *most important* and oldest celebration of the Christian Church. At Easter, Christians celebrate the resurrection of Jesus Christ. This is the defining event in all of history for Christians. The date for Easter changes each year. Easter is held between March 21 and April 25 on the first Sunday after the first full moon following the northern spring equinox.

Here's another interesting fact. In the Bible, Easter is described in vivid detail in all four Gospels. Christmas, in contrast, is discussed in only two Gospels. This says something about the relative importance of Christmas and Easter for Christians. Easter is, by far, more important. Easter is resurrection of Jesus who died for our sins that we might be reconciled with Almighty God. Easter is, by far, the most important Christian holiday.

Another interesting fact: The word *Easter* stems from *Eostre* (*or* Ishtar or Astarte). It is the name of a Pagan goddess of fertility celebrated during the spring solstice. This was a Pagan Anglo-Saxon Goddess. This mythical figure is said to have been the goddess of the sunrise and the spring. The bunnies and eggs we use to celebrate Easter today stem from the fact that these things symbolize the new growth associated with Spring. She is also the Teutonic goddess of the dawn and the direction of the dawn sunrise, East, is named for her. In Norse mythology, the name is spelled *Eostare*.

So why is the Christian holiday named after a Pagan goddess? First of all, almost all tribal peoples the world over celebrated the coming of spring as this meant the beginning of the planting season and of an eventual bounty of food. Thus, spring was worth celebrating. Next when Christians were spreading the Gospel of Jesus during the Middle Ages, they frequently adapted (borrowed or stole) older nonChristian celebrations and re- interpreted them as Christian. That was the case with Easter.

Another interesting fact: Jesus never celebrated Easter in his lifetime (of course, he never celebrated Christmas either). Rather, Jesus celebrated all the traditional Jewish holidays, one of which is Passover.

Read Luke 22:7–14. This passage shows that the event Christians known as the Last Supper was actually a Jewish celebration of Passover. Jesus had ordered his disciples to prepare a pass over meal for he and his followers.

Now Passover for Jesus and all Jews was the celebration and anniversary of the day God delivered them out of Egyptian bondage. To punish the Egyptian king, God intended to kill the first-born male in every household in Egypt. However, God promised to pass over houses of Jewish families, so he passed over any house with the blood of a perfect lamb smeared on its doorpost. God then commanded the Jews to remember their deliverance through the ceremony of the Passover.

Passover comes in the spring each year. Thus, Jesus was celebrating Passover during the meal Christians call the "Last Supper." Both the cup and the unleavened bread used for communion were a traditional part of the Jewish Passover feast.

So Why Do We Celebrate Easter?

The simple answer is, Christ commanded it. Read Matthew 26:26–29 and Mark 14:22–25. Now for just a moment, imagine the disciples on that day. How would it feel if someone you have been following for three years suddenly says they will never eat again in this world? That you cannot follow him anymore? Now read John 13:36–14:4. In this passage, we see confusion from the disciples. Why couldn't they follow Jesus like they'd been doing so long? Where was Jesus going that they could not follow him? He was going to his glory, the first Easter!

In the Christian view, the sacrificial lamb of the Jewish Passover (the lamb from which the blood painted on the door came) has now become Jesus. Jesus is our sacrificial Lamb. He chose to sacrifice himself for our sins in order to rebuild our right relationship with God. If we accept the gift of his sacrifice, then his blood is believed to have saved us from our own sin. Thus, Easter is the *Christian Passover*. Jesus is our sacrifice!

> For all have sinned, and come short of the glory of God (Romans 3:23).
>
> For the wages of sin is death, but the gift of God is eternal life in Christ Jesus our Lord (Romans 6:23).

That gift of God referred to above in simple terms is Easter! To understand Jesus's sacrifice, we must remember that Jesus chose to experience that torture and to die that horrible death in order to become a sacrifice for our sins—mine and yours. In Jesus's death and resurrection, lay our very lives. Jesus's sacrifice, his self-chosen death on the cross, made it possible for us to have an unblemished relationship with God once again.

Thus, Jesus's sacrifice is the whole ball game! Easter or Jesus's sacrifice is the essence of Christian belief:

- that God entered history, at a certain point in time that God experienced life just as I do, or as you do
- that God knew failures and successes, believers, and betrayal, and
- that he chose to experience the greatest torture ever experienced by anyone, for us
- Jesus then conquered them all, including death, through his resurrection, and promised for all believers, a life everlasting.

> But God commended his love toward us, in that, while we were yet sinners, Christ died for us (Romans 5:8).

> For whosoever shall call upon the name of the Lord shall be saved (Romans 10:13).

Easter is the good news of the Gospel—the good news of Easter morning. God loves us so much that he offered his only begotten Son, Jesus, to pay our sin debt for us. This gift is available to us all. When we chose to believe that the man Jesus suffered and died for us to pay our debt personally, we can have inner peace and an eternal life. At the exact moment that we believe in what Jesus did on the cross for us, our life changes. It is a choice.

Christ's Righteousness

Another way to consider the meaning of Easter is to consider who God sees when he looks at you and me, even we Rogue Warriors, we broken people. Christ's righteousness is the name of this concept. At the cross, Jesus took our sins upon himself, leaving us blameless before God. This is why so many old Christian hymns refer to Jesus *washing away our sins* and leaving us *whiter than snow, Lord.* They speak of the *power in the blood!*

Thus, when God looks at you, even sitting there in that jail cell or halfway house, he doesn't see an addict or a criminal. He doesn't see brokenness. Rather, when God looks at you, a Christian believer, and a Jesus follower, he sees Jesus's righteousness.

God sees a man who walked on water. He looks at you and sees a man who raised Lazarus from the dead, who turned water into wine at the wedding feast in Cana, and he sees a man of such great love and compassion that he chose to sacrifice himself for others. We are indeed blessed because Jesus's sacrifice made us right with God again!

Summary

So what does Easter mean? Is it bunnies and eggs or something more? For Christians, Easter is everything! At Easter, when we talk of the stone that was rolled away or the blessed Easter morning, we most clearly sense that we are blessed by the righteousness of Jesus. God Almighty looks at you and me and sees not our sin but the righteousness and purity of Jesus. Our sins, no matter what they may be, even for those of us who are broken, have been replaced with God's grace! We are no longer guilty! We have the righteousness of Jesus! That's a very powerful thought when you really sit and contemplate it.

So I'll ask you to do just that, guys. For all of the coming week, read these passages above in a quiet moment or two and think about what Easter means, what Christ righteousness means for us all. Then next Sunday, we'll gather again, and together, we shall indeed have a blessed Easter!

Continuing Your Journey to God

So there you are, still sitting right there, looking at this book just like when you started reading the introduction many days or weeks ago. You're probably still sitting alone. Maybe you are sitting at home or in a bedroom of a halfway house somewhere—maybe a local lockup. It doesn't matter where you are. It only matters what you do in response to this book.

If you've read this far all the way to the end, something has probably changed, something deep inside of you might be different. By reading this—just by reading this book, you've probably changed! If, in using this book, you have decided to follow Jesus, you are now made new! The plain fact is you would not have continued reading, unless this book was speaking to you in some way.

So now for the introductions. That's Jesus, the one right there with you right now. He's inside you, he's also beside you, and all around you! He is everywhere and in all things including you. You may not realize it, but you probably hear his voice inside all the time—that still, small voice saying get away from those folks still in the drug lifestyle, or come into my house this Sunday morning and you'll feel better all week! That voice inside you telling you that you are worthy of love no matter your situation on this earth.

So how do you respond to this? What do you do now, sitting there on your bed or chair? That answer will be different for all of us, but I can make one suggestion.

Talk a bit more to Jesus. Like I said at the beginning, don't make up what you might think of as grand words. Just talk to your friend and your Lord. He is sitting right there beside you. He is behind you and inside of you. You might as well talk with your friend. In fact, you would do well if you chose to know him much better.

If you do, your life will be changed forever. You will no longer be broken. You will be made whole! This is the promise of God.

From one broken person to another, may God bless you always.

Billy

ABOUT THE AUTHOR

William N. Bender is a committed Christian who was also a history major and student of Christianity as an undergraduate at St. Andrews Presbyterian College. He attained his Ph.D in 1983 from the University of North Carolina and taught in higher education around the nation for twenty-six years. He has previously published 47 books for educators and four historic fiction novels, each with a spiritual focus. These may be obtained by contacting the publisher: Currahee Books, 171 Laurel Mt. Drive, Toccoa, GA 30577. He has conducted many workshops for educators during his career, and at this point, he is writing a book each year. His work reflected herein stems from many years of experience working with adolescents and young adults from dysfunctional families, and many men from half-way houses over the years.